Northwest Passage

Northwest Passage

The Early Years of Ellis Scism,
1909-1949
by Ellis Scism with Stanley Scism

Northwest Passage:
The Early Years of Ellis Scism, 1909–1949

by Ellis Scism with Stanley Scism

©1994 by Stanley Scism
Hazelwood, MO 63042-2299

Printed in the United States of America.

Scism, Ellis, d. 1994.
    Northwest passage : the early years of Ellis Scism, 1909-1949 / by Ellis Scism with Stanley Scism.
       p.   cm.
    ISBN 1-56722-023-1
    1. Scism, Ellis, d. 1994. 2. United Pentecostal Church International—Clergy—Biography. 3. United Pentecostal Church International—Missions—India. 4. United Pentecostal Church—India—History. 5. India—Church history. 6. Missionaries—United States—Biography. 7. Missionaries—India—Biography. I. Scism, Stanley, 1958- . II. Title
    BX8777.5.S34 1994
    289.9'4'092—dc20
    [B]   94-12003
                                         CIP

To John and Grace Scism,
parents and great-grandparents

Contents

Foreword

During a recent visit to India I visited the town of Adur and stayed in the very bungalow where Ellis and Marjorie Scism lived most of their seventeen years in India. In this hot, tropical setting where comforts of life known to the Westerner are few and far between, I relived many experiences with my father and mother. Their lives of tremendous sacrifice and willingness to face untold hardship for the sake of the gospel have made a profound impact on the lives of literally thousands of people.

Beginning their missionary work in India with some 300 people, they departed India leaving a church of over 30,000 members.

What kind of life and background help prepare a man for this tremendous challenge? From where do these qualities of life emanate?

The oncologist working with my father on more than one occasion stated, "This man is most remarkable! A movie should be made of his life, so that the world may know of his greatness."

How thankful I am that my father and my son have worked together many long hours to bring to us the story of Ellis Scism from his birth up to his India mission. (The story of his life and work in India will follow in a second volume.) In *Northwest Passage* you will find some of those secrets of strength that helped shape this man of determination and valor. Long before his departure for India, these qualities of a successful life were already evident.

Born in humble circumstances, Ellis Scism has always been very grateful for every kindness shown and all blessings received. Never has he indicated a desire for credit for the many accomplishments. Rather he has always in genuine humility given the glory to God. Thank you, Dad, for being such a tremendous example of a real Christian.

Your loving son,
Harry

$\mathcal{P}$reface

Many people have suggested that I write this book. I can only thank the following for helping me:

God, for the breath and strength to write.

Harry and Audrene Scism for building in me a respect for my grandparents.

Ellis and Marjorie Scism, Milba and Verna Hruza for lives that deserve such respect.

Ellis Scism for helping me by taping his memories when they would occur to him, and for sitting, even when weak physically, for hours to answer my questions.

John Klemin for providing the files and minutes for Ellis Scism's years as district superintendent in the Northwest.

C. H. Yadon for presenting his memories of Ellis Scism's early ministerial years. He tied them together with the theme, "The steps of a good man are ordered by the LORD" (Psalm 37:23), and the statement, "When I think of that, I think of Ellis Scism."

Ferne Scism Ackley, Philip Long, and especially Ronna Cross for hours of work transcribing tapes.

Kenneth Reeves and the First United Pentecostal Church in Granite City, Illinois, for the money to buy the computer I used in writing this book.

Mary Wallace for looking over the manuscript and offering suggestions. Any errors are, of course, mine.

Brian Crain, Bill Smeltzer, and Richard Frank for helping on those computer details which befuddle me. Kent Curry for printing the document on his printer so that I could present it for publication. Word Aflame Press for publishing it, Margie McNall, Tim Agnew and Virginia Rigdon for their aid.

Ellis Scism has lived a long and very busy life in many places. I welcome the recorded or written memories of anyone. You may send them directly to me or in care of the publisher.

Stanley Scism
3749 Red Hawk Court
Bridgeton, MO 63044

Prologue

During the ninth to eleventh centuries A.D., Norsemen came plundering into the rest of Europe. While the Swedes tended to raid central and eastern Europe, the Norwegians and Danes usually traveled west and southwest, eventually many of them settling in northern France and giving this new home their name—Normandy.

When William the Conqueror successfully asserted his claim to the English throne in 1066, he brought with him various Norman knights, including the Chisholms, who became a Scottish clan and lived in the Scottish lowlands until they acquired lands by marriage in the highland regions of Erchless and Strathglass. In 1359, Sir Robert was appointed Constable of the nearby great Royal Castle of Urquhart, best known to Americans as the most common site of Loch Ness monster sightings.

In the 1600s, some of the more indifferently educated Chisholms migrated to Ulster, in the process probably carelessly spelling their name. In the very early 1700s, a man who spelled his name Sism owned a small farm in County Antrim, Northern Ireland—the part of Ireland nearest Scotland.

In 1729, the Scisms crossed the Atlantic Ocean, landing in Philadelphia, the colonies' largest city at the time. William Scism was born in Virginia in 1776 and begat Jesse in 1809, who begat James in 1834, who begat John, his fifth son, in 1876. During these years, the family moved from Virginia to North Carolina to Tennessee to Stoddard County, Missouri.

When John was eighteen, James moved his family to Hilltop, near Harrison, Arkansas. John and his friends would ride their horses past brush arbor meetings, firing their revolvers, then gallop off into the woods. When the sheriff's posse would gallop by, the young men would hold their horses' nostrils to prevent them from whinnying while the other horses passed by. When the posse had thundered out of earshot, the young men would ride back to the brush arbor and fire off their revolvers some more.

Because this behavior kept John in the sheriff's bad books and because one of John's older brothers, Bob, had already moved out to Oregon and found it good, James Scism in 1894 packed up his family and their belongings and left Arkansas by covered wagon, heading for Oregon. They had to work in Texas along the way to save up enough money for the rest of the journey, but they finally reached Oregon.

James was known in the family as being very even-tempered—angry all the time. Later, his mind began to slip, and when he heard about a new gold rush in California, he left Oregon from a wayside station by train with a shovel in hand. Apparently, he left the train at another wayside station in California and started off on foot. He was found in quicksand. There was some suspicion of foul play, but it was never proven. His body was brought back to North Howell.

In Oregon, his son John met a young lady named Grace Eleanor Webb, who attracted his attention. Later, while she visited friends in Colfax, Washington, John visited her.

14

They married across the state line in Stites, northern Idaho, probably in 1903. John then briefly worked in northern Idaho timber with his brother, Bob, after which they all moved back to the Howell area near Salem, Oregon. John and Grace begat Ellis, their second son, in 1909. And here our story begins.

CHAPTER ONE

North Howell Home

$\mathcal{I}$ was born on the Opadahl Place in Central Howell, east-northeast of Salem, Oregon. My mother came from the well-known Webb family, who had settled about ten miles away in Gervais long before on a donation land claim. They now lived in Silverton. Mother's maternal grandfather, a Thurmond, had lived in different homes in the general area, including McMinnville, for many years. (Gervais, Silverton, and McMinnville all are towns near Howell.)

Ray, my older brother, was born in 1905, and still lives at this writing. A sister, Pearl, born in 1907, lived only eleven months. Perhaps Mother wanted a girl after her grief over Pearl's death, because after my birth she briefly dressed me up in girls' clothes and kept my hair long. I'd get my hair caught in briars and weeds and want her to cut it. However, maybe she didn't necessarily want a girl—

many parents of that time did this with their baby boys.

My father's father had already died when I was born, and Dad's mother lived in Scotts Mills with her daughter, my Aunt Elizabeth. Sherman, Weston, and Oscar Howard, first cousins of mine, lived with their mother, Molly, one of Dad's older sisters. Dad would tell us stories about Molly's girlhood in the Missouri Ozarks. Apparently, her schoolteacher in Arkansas once remonstrated and reprimanded her very strongly regarding stepping on top of the benches to walk back to her bench. Back then, the benches were just logs cut in half, with holes bored in each end to hold poles that were the bench's legs. There were no desks; the children held their papers on their laps or worked on the same surface they sat on. Molly had a rather stubborn nature and walked back to her bench the same way she had the first time, even though the teacher would threaten to use the shillelagh.

Dad told Ray and me stories about the community he had grown up in:

One man hung around a general store sifting the gunpowder, which was sold in big boxes, through his fingers. He apparently liked the feel of it, for he asked the shopkeeper, "How much a grab?" (Gunpowder was sold by the fistful.) After the shopkeeper said, "Ten cents a grab," the man stood up, slapped a dime on the counter, grabbed the whole box, and ran out of the store.

One lady brought her home-churned butter to the local general store to be wrapped and sold. A mouse had gotten into her cream, but since she could not afford to lose it, she concluded that she should take the shopkeeper into her confidence, explain what had happened, and say, "What you don't know won't hurt you." He could sell it to someone else who wouldn't know about the mouse.

The shopkeeper took this butter to the back room, wrapped it in one of his wrappers, brought it back, gave it to her, and said "Well, it's surrre true—what you don't know won't hurt you." The result: she took her own butter back home and, I hope, enjoyed it.

A man who held a mutual grudge with a local general storekeeper came in one day and announced, "I bet you fifty cents I can step in that big tub of eggs and not break one." Local farmers selling eggs to the general storekeeper would place them in the tub, from which customers could pick them out. The shopkeeper, apparently thinking this man must be some sort of fool to wager so large a sum on something so impossible, took him up on the bet. The man stepped into the tub in his big rubber work boots and tromped back and forth until he had broken every single egg in the tub. He then stepped out of the tub, slopping egg yolk all over the floor, squished and slithered his way up to the counter, slapped fifty cents on the counter, and cheerfully proclaimed, "You won the bet! You beat me hands down!" Then he left the store the same way he had left the tub—with long, messy bootprints to the door. The yolk was on the manager.

Dad had experienced plenty himself:

One day as a very young boy, he happened to look in a brush arbor to see a young man and young lady sitting up near the front. He and his friends crawled under the plank benches so that they could hear what might be said, in time to hear the young man telling the young lady how much he loved her and that he could not carry on his days without her responding to his concern. After a while he finished, followed by quite a pause. Finally she said, "Well,

I'm sorry, but that's more than I can say for you." Without missing a beat, he responded, "Not if you could lie like I did."

During Dad's boyhood days, school was conducted only three months of the year—the hottest three months, as he said, when no one could learn anything anyway.

One day as he sat on his bench, he kept swinging one of his legs back and forth, back and forth. It felt so good that he swung it farther until finally he kicked the boy in front of him on the floor. The teacher wanted to know what had happened to him. Apparently the school didn't have too much discipline.

One schoolteacher possessed both a very lovely pocket watch and also some very patched, ragged trousers. This teacher once scheduled a "literary"—an event featuring student literature readings and recitations before a gathering of parents, teachers, and students. John, having been asked to recite a poem, presented one of his own composition:

> I viewed you up, I viewed you down;
> I compared your poverty with your riches.
> I decided you'd better sell your watch
> And buy yourself a pair of britches.

This created a stir, and the teacher wanted to shake up John in a rather demonstrative way, but some of the older students (some students stayed in school much longer than they do in today's educational system) wouldn't let him give John any difficulty.

At another literary, John was asked to speak a piece, so he recited another of his creations:

Lord, have mercy on us poor scholars!
They hired a fool
To teach the school
And are paying him seventy dollars!

That schoolmaster was also very persuaded to correct John's ways, but people prevailed upon him and he did not carry out his threats.

After they moved to Arkansas, at a shouting, rip-roaring brush arbor meeting he attended, one of the young men in the group said, "I wish so-and-so was here." Another young man said, "I do, too! He took my girlfriend home."

Also when he was a young man, John and some others went to a meeting in a log church building. These young fellows, all curiosity, tried to listen to what was going on inside the building. One young man put his eye right up to where a little bit of chinking had come out from between the logs. At that moment, someone inside—the good Lord knows who—spit tobacco juice right through the crack dead center and hit the young fellow in the eye. Of course, tobacco juice stings terribly, so he rolled on the ground with pain. The other fellows naturally all felt for him, but they still had a bit of merriment at his expense.

While the family was traveling West toward Oregon, they would stop along the way, get a job, work a while, save up money, then continue. At one of these stops in Texas, while they lived in a line house, some of my father's brothers split up some stove wood, then noticed that someone had been stealing their wood. One brother would come out to the front porch, where the firewood was stacked, early in the morning and discover that someone had been there before him. Several logs that had been there the previous evening were now gone.

After several mornings of this, he selected an ordinary-looking log, such as a thief might think wouldn't be missed, and with an auger bored a hole in the end of it. This hole he filled with gunpowder, then stopped up the end of the hole with sawdust and marked the log so that he wouldn't select it for his own fire. Early the next morning, a neighbor's stove not too far away blew up. That stopped the firewood thievery and located the thief.

On these stories, Ray and I lived. We moved from the Opadahl Place in Central Howell to North Howell when I was very young, so I do not recall our move and must rely on what my parents have told me. The North Howell community contained many German-speaking people who had settled in the area long before. They figured heavily in my childhood. Adam Reznicsek, the father of one of these families, was quite instrumental in community prayer meetings. He and his wife had six sons—Joe, Rafel, Adam Jr., Albert, Valentine, and Abraham—and two daughters—Anna and Mary. Mary died at a very young age in a fire. Joe, thirteen years older than I, became my good friend and hero.

Dad visited Idaho looking for work and found a job. We all moved there. First Dad worked for Sam Scism, a big farmer and distant cousin who lived on Missouri Road a few miles from Nampa, Idaho, and later with a crew who dug irrigation canal trenches and laid power lines through that area.

Ray was already a fighter and scrapper. Later he served in the military and, after that, was a policeman. In Idaho, he got in trouble with a Basque sheepherder, probably by fighting with one of his children. Dad felt it necessary to buy a .38 Smith and Wesson revolver to protect his son from the sheepherder Basqueing in rage.

When the Idaho job ended, we moved back to North Howell in Oregon and stayed at Uncle Bob's place briefly until we rented a house across the ravine from his. A creek flowed through the ravine, and the main road ran beside the ravine on Uncle Bob's side.

One day, while my brother and I (I was now about five years old) played with a wagon in the dusty road, Mrs. Stephens, who lived in the community, opened the gate, walked in the house and invited Mother to a church meeting in her house that night to hear a visiting Jamaican preacher, Brother Frey. Mrs. Stephens, famous in the community as "The Neighborhood Gazette" because she knew everything going on and gossiped, did not claim to be a Christian. My parents suspected that she simply wanted more people in her house for her meeting than any other neighbors had for theirs. Nevertheless, Mother accepted. She had been a member of the hard-shell Missionary Baptist Church, and so was inclined toward religion.

That night, people came from many homes and many extended families. Everyone was there—the Reznicseks, the Ditchens, the Pfaus, the Schmidts, the Sanns, and our whole family—Dad and Mom, Ray and I, Dad's sister and Uncle Bob, Uncle Bob's son Ike, and Ike's wife. The meeting began. We had no electric lights, just a little old-fashioned kerosene light sitting on a tall, two-foot-square, four-legged table. The adults sat on chairs, and we boys sat on wash benches (benches you set a tub on as you scrubbed clothes by hand) and whatever else the Stephenses had.

After the considerably exuberant singing, Brother Frey began preaching. During his sermon, Ike and his wife stood up to go. Brother Frey asked them why they were leaving. Ike said his wife had a severe migraine headache. (She had these often. She would have to lie very still and not raise her head off the pillow.) Brother Frey perfunctorily tossed his Bible on the stand. The light flickered. He walked over to her, laid his hands on her head without waiting to ask whether she wanted this or not, and prayed for God to heal her headache. Neither Ike nor his wife had given their hearts to Jesus Christ, nor did they ever. Then the preacher asked if her head ached. She said no.

Dad laughed. He thought this preacher was just trying to pull something over on the people, and that Ike's wife was tricking him with this ruse so that she could go home. The preacher said, "O fools, to see the power of God and to laugh at it!" That sobered Dad up.

Ike's wife never had migraines again. God showed her His grace, favor, and mercy even though her attitude showed no reciprocal thanksgiving. Until she passed away, she still lived the way she had before.

During that meeting, some unusual happenings witnessed to Dad about God's power. He knew about Baptist and Methodist brush arbor meetings in the South, and these hadn't particularly impressed him, but he also knew all about Ike's wife's headaches. This was our first contact with and interest in Pentecostal Christianity.

Nevertheless, my father still did not give his heart to the Lord at all. He was a good man but, of course, not perfect. He needed to repent and give himself to Jesus, but he indicated no interest or inclination, although his mother had gently admonished him to appreciate church and religious services. Appreciation of God was not his lifestyle, especially after he left Arkansas and went West.

After a number of meetings held in community homes with Brother Frey speaking, some people wanted a tent meeting in a beautiful oak grove on a farm my father rented from John Thurmond, my mother's uncle. Mother, who had already received the Holy Spirit, interceded and spoke to Dad, who spoke to John Thurmond. John Thurmond told John Scism, "John, as long as you'll be responsible for it and see that everything goes all right, it's all right with me." As a result, the Pentecostal people pitched their tent in this beautiful oak grove on one corner of the farm in a very prominent place in the community. They had some wonderful meetings.

The old-fashioned tent had one center pole and an outside rope. Two gas mantle lights were strung up inside—one above the platform and the other over the main audience. Straw covered the ground. Of course, the people had no canvas fireproofing or other modern fire precautions, but the Lord met them there and a number of people came to Him. The meetings accomplished much for God. Brother Frey preached wonderfully and really knew how to pray. I heard him pray many times and his prayer and ministry affected me, even though I was just a small boy.

But the meetings met opposition and, before they closed, one group came to harass us. They planned to cut the outside rope that held up the tent. This activated Dad as nothing else had yet, because he had accepted responsibility for the property's safety. He knew that if the tent rope were cut, the tent would collapse, the lamps would fall into the straw and start a fire. The people would be trapped in the tent and probably burned alive. The damage would affect not only property, but also life. The situation was so bad that Dad went to the house and brought back his .38 Smith and Wesson revolver. He walked up to the ringleader of the group, with Uncle Bob and his jackknife right behind. Pete Schmidt, also present, climbed a tree.

Dad stood in front of the ringleader, placed his finger on his own nose, and said, "Hit me here." Of course, the young man didn't, because Dad had already turned white with rage and the ringleader knew that if he hit Dad, Dad would shoot him. Since following Dad's request was not the thing to do, they left. As a result, Dad protected the Pentecostal people at a time when he wasn't yet one himself.

Although Brother Frey could preach and pray until you would think that heaven was just a few feet above the tent, in the end his ministry was worthless because he would sometimes borrow a horse and a buggy, take me along as a decoy (I was very small and totally unaware of this role until long afterward), and go to where an old lake had been drained off, to meet another brother's wife. Later, he came to my dad and apologized, admitting he had done wrong. That was the end of Brother Frey's ministry.

Yet, even though Brother Frey turned out not to be the man he was supposed to be, should have been, and could have been, yet without question he at one time knew God and the Bible in the spiritual illumination he had then. (This was 1914. We had heard nothing about the doctrine of Oneness; these were "Council days" before the Assemblies of God was formed.)

Some time later, they closed the convention, struck the tent, went back to house meetings as they had before. In the home of the Rezniczeks about a year later, Dad repented and surrendered his heart to the Lord. He still had not been baptized with the Holy Spirit, but he had made a start for the Lord.

John Scism (sitting in the back) on the work crew for Nampa, Idaho. They dug trenches for irrigation canals and strung up wires for electricity all through the Nampa-Caldwell-Boise area.

Ellis Scism and his mother, Grace.

Ellis Scism and his father, John.

Ellis in North Howell (1910?) at a tender age. A beautiful baby who every six months took a turn for the worse according to his father, John.

Ellis Scism

CHAPTER TWO

Scism Road

When I was about seven or eight, Dad bought about eighteen acres of quite heavily wooded land on a side road, now a town street called Scism Road but then a private road a few miles from the main road, way back in the interior timber, Of course, in the beginning the whole Pacific Northwest was timber, and by the time I came along, much of it still was.

To build this log house, Dad had to clear some land. This was called "grubbing the area." First he cut down many second-growth trees to create room to build a house, then trimmed the logs with an axe and faced them with an adze (a broad, flat-bladed axe). To face means to flatten one side of a log. We didn't plane this surface—we had no planes in those days. Then he nailed boards against these logs and pasted or tacked felt paper against the boards. The rough lumber was very convenient in building such a house. No particular chinking closed up cracks between the logs as they had in the old days down in Arkansas where Dad came from. Dad just nailed some shakes (hand-made shingles) between the logs, in some spots wadding up newspaper or other paper before nailing on the shakes.

The place was quite large and very roughly done—nothing compared to our modern homes. It wasn't much to look at, but it was home and, after having moved for so many years, the family enjoyed having a place to call home. We lived there through much of my childhood, and I remember seeing a Bible in that home when I was quite young.

We had no sawn rafters in our home—just three-inch-diameter poles Dad had peeled. These poles supported crosspieces, on which Dad nailed shakes. Dad made shakes with a froe (an L-shaped tool consisting of a blade about three inches wide and twelve to fifteen inches long, attached to an eighteen-inch handle). Dad hammered the froe into the wood, then pried the wood apart, using the froe handle. If the shake was turning out too small, he knocked one end of the froe further down into the wood. The average shake was six or seven inches wide and two feet long.

One year in the early '20s, we had a tremendously heavy snow—twenty-four or twenty-five inches. One night I heard scraping sounds on the roof. Dad was working outside. The snow on the roof was so heavy that the roof was beginning to creak and there was a danger of it falling in. Dad had nailed a long rod perpendicular to a board and was outside pulling the snow off the shake roof onto the ground.

Many years later, after I married and had children and

had been pastoring, Marjorie and I moved to Salem to help take care of Mother and Dad. Harry was quite a small boy, and Ferne was a toddler. That must have been around 1937. We had around thirty-one inches of snow on the level. Those were the two heaviest snows we experienced in Oregon during my years there.

Close to the old log house, some trees still stood. One time, we had a very heavy rain. A strong wind came along, and during the night something hit the end of the house, creating quite a commotion. When we went outside to look, we found out that one of these trees had fallen. (Fir trees do not have a taproot.) The top of the tree had broken the overhanging part of the roof beyond the gable wall, then had scraped down the end of the log house. I don't think that part of the roof was ever repaired.

Clearing the rest of the land and selling the wood provided my father with his living. One old man named Connor used to work for my dad as a woodcutter. Dad paid him by the cord (a stack of logs four feet wide and high and eight feet long).

Dad built Connor a little one-room cabin. In it he had a little kitchen stove to cook on. His heating arrangement consisted of logs cut in half and placed in the middle of the room to form a border, filled inside with dirt. A funnel-shaped cone helped him build a fire for heat. Naturally, his cabin was filled with smoke, but that did not seem to bother him.

Connor had lived with Indians as a boy, and when we were boys, my brother and I would sit with him while he told us stories of happenings during his younger life with the Indians. He made two bows, one for my brother and one for me, out of yew. In fact, I still had mine until it broke during my move from Portland to St. Louis in 1983. He had tempered and bent it just right. We kids played with these when we played Indians.

Finally we grubbed out quite a bit of space, raised some crops, and had a large garden near the house. Harvesting all the timber, first and second growth, took years. I participated in some of this work full time after graduating from eighth grade.

When I was very young, the country road crew came with their wagons and teams of horses, clearing the forest for a road. They would cut down the trees, pull out the stumps, and spread dirt about four inches thick with a hump in the middle to encourage drainage.

My father was a great hand at dealing horses. He liked to trade horses and traded often, though he didn't have much to trade with. Anyway he enjoyed it and was pretty good at judging horses. Sometimes he would come out very well and sometimes not so well.

When I was six or seven, Dad had a corral built outside the barn where he used to keep horses. Dad and my brother would put hay in a bin to feed the horses. All this was surrounded by a fence. Dad had told me not to go among the horses, but I liked horses, so one day, when I saw a horse feeding in the corral, I went in there, crawled up on the manger, and put my arm up over its mane.

When I came to, I was lying on the ground with my arm over the stump of a little second-growth tree. The stump was sharp because the tree had been cut down with an axe. My arm had a bulge, so, even though the bone hadn't broken through the skin, I knew it was broken. I also knew that I had disobeyed Dad and that I had to go to him and confess my fault

After I had sat for a while by another stump, I went into the house and told my parents and my cousin, Oscar Howard, who was there, what had happened. They prayed for me, and I felt the bone just scrape back together again. I never did go to a doctor to have it set. The folks put some splints around it and wrapped it. My arm still is not exactly as it was originally—the elbow is shaped a little differently on that arm, which reminds me of what happened long, long ago, and of the price one pays for disobedience.

Maybe I came honestly by my stubbornness about horses. Cousin Ike was a very quick-tempered man in some respects and had a horse that gave him much trouble. One day, he became so displeased with this horse that he hit it over the head with a stick and knocked it out. It fell to the ground. Cousin Ike was so perturbed that he just sat down on its head, which was not a very wise thing to do. While he was sitting there, the horse came to and somehow kicked him, cracking one of his ribs. He never did forget that. Of course, he was more displeased than ever to think a dumb animal would be able to give him such a whack as to crack a rib, but he'd paid a price for his quick temper. Keeping horses can be costly, considering all the prices involved.

In the midst of all these equine events, we kept attending church. Our community sometimes held weekday evening meetings and always held Sunday afternoon services in various homes, very often led by old Brother Adam Reznicsek. Back then, after the afternoon service, some of the folks would go home to take care of the stock, seeing that they were fed, watered, cared for, and milked. Then these people would return and we would all have our evening meal together around a table, followed by a night service. These were not large groups; our commuity was small. After the meeting, we'd walk home at night on the muddy roads. I gave my heart to the Lord when I was just six or seven in one of these prayer meetings, led by Brother Voget.

The day finally came when, because I was seven and going into school as a first grader, the lower-grades teacher, Miss Rouse, would spend one night at our house. At the beginning of each school year, she would visit each family who was sending a new student to her classroom. This very good gesture on her part helped acquaint her with the parents in the community, which in turn helped her better understand and teach the children in her class. (Another lady taught grades five through eight in the school's other classroom.) When Miss Rouse came to our house, she wanted me to sit on her lap, which I most obediently did. As a youngster, I approved of and enjoyed her visit to our home, and I know my father, mother, and brother did as well.

We had to walk about two and a half miles, even with shortcuts, to the North Howell School, an old building even in those days. The ground floor sat somewhat high, with a wood-storage area underneath. Because my brother was four years my senior, we often walked together to school, and he watched out for his little brother.

Some of the neighborhood boys disliked my brother very much at times. Many of these boys were of German, Austrian, or Hungarian descent—their parents had come over long ago from the old country. In World War I America fought against Germany and the Austro-Hungarian Empire. Sometimes the boys would have fights on the shortcuts to and from school. (The dusty main road went around the field fences, so we cut through farms and wooded areas.)

Once, on a day I missed school, Ray took the road, but several of the German boys somewhat perturbed with Ray had decided to gang up on him, so they stretched a wire across the road. They covered it with dust and leaves, attached one end to a fence post, and hid on the other side in the bushes where he couldn't see them. When he stepped over the wire, they yanked it tight to trip him so that they could pile on him after he fell. It almost worked. He stumbled but regained his balance. When it was over, they had a bit of a trouncing themselves because he could handle himself quite well in those days. In fact, he had considerable experience in this type of thing.

Once an older student tried to take a baseball bat away from me. While we were each tugging at it, Ray came up, and apparently thinking that I was going to let go of the handle, said, "Don't give it to him!" I said, "Don't worry, I'll give it to him," wrenched the bat out of the other boy's hands, and cracked him across the shins with it. Now that was courageous of me, wasn't it? But not very spiritual.

Still, although we boys occasionally experienced breakdowns in our community feeling, as the years came and went we had good times together. The school was a good one, too. I went there for five years until we moved to Silverton.

Once while we knelt in a prayer meeting when I was about eight years old, I felt that the Lord had told me to read the twenty-fifth chapter of John. After prayer ended and everyone sat up, old Brother Reznicsek asked me, "Ellis, what chapter shall we read tonight?" Assuming that the Lord had spoken to me, I informed him that we should read John chapter twenty-five. I also shared how good the Lord had been to tell me that we should read it, and about how I had thought I should read it later on, but here I was having an opportunity to hear it read right during the meeting itself. Of course, he knew that The Gospel According to John does not have twenty-five chapters, but while leafing through his Bible he commented that, though he didn't think John had twenty-five chapters, he would look and see what he could read. He was letting me down easily. Of course, we found out that John does not have twenty-five chapters. This experience has greatly helped me through the years to realize that not every voice we hear really comes from God—God's Spirit doesn't sponsor and God's presence doesn't motivate *every* impression we receive.

But some He does. For example, when I was a boy we used to go to the Howards' place for prayer meetings or church services from time to time. Sherman and Weston were already gone and in the military, but I remember Oscar sitting on an old, rawhide-bottom chair and quivering under the power of conviction—beads of perspiration all over his forehead and face, stubbornly resisting and not yielding to God's Spirit. Later on, he did yield before he followed his brothers into the service.

When I was eight or nine, my Uncle Bob gave me a little runt pig out of a litter he had. I took it home and cared for it as best I could. When the time came a few months later to butcher the litter, the former runt was bigger and fatter than all the other pigs. I took great boyhood pleasure in my pig's weighing so much more than those raised by Uncle Bob and Ike.

People killed pigs differently then from what they do in many places today. The old-fashioned way was to shoot the pig, stick it, or knock it on the head. Then they put it into a big vat of hot scalding water, where they scraped off the hair.

Sometimes our family would visit Grandpa and Grandma Webb in Silverton. I would lie in front of the fireplace, watching the fire. It never did throw out much heat, but it was always fascinating to look at.

Grandfather Webb took Ray and me for an outing to Pacific City on the coast when I was eight or nine. Grandpa came from his nice home in Silverton to our log house in North Howell, driving his Model T Ford. I don't remember if Grandmother stayed with Mother or not, but we three went to the coast on the roads of mixed dirt and gravel.

We arrived at Pacific City and Grandpa pitched the tent. We prepared the campsite, then started looking around for firewood to cook with. Grandpa spied a piece of planking and cut it up to build a fire. Other people had camped in the same area; apparently Grandpa had taken someone else's planking. They made inquiry about that, but Grandad had already cut up the wood. Everything worked out all right, though the other camper was somewhat sorry for what had happened to the planking that he had brought for himself. Going out to the coast with Grandad was really a highlight because we did not have many such trips.

We lived in an area without electricity, so our washing machine was hand operated. Since our surface well was not very deep, on wash day we had to go down to the creek, where we had a spring, and pack water up to the

37

house, usually in five-gallon kerosene tins or in buckets. I have often thought that packing water might have something to do with my left shoulder being a little longer than my right.

None of us, especially me, looked forward to wash day. Our washing machine had a handle to push back and forth to help the gyrator run. This seemingly never-ending job was usually my privilege when I was about nine or ten.

Dad bought another horse—George. He was gray and had something wrong with his hind legs—a little hamstrung. While George was with us, Gladys Neeley came to visit my folks. Dad had known her when she taught my brother first grade in Idaho at Deer Flat. In fact, she and Dad had danced there before either of them came to know the Lord. That school was later named Scism School, after other relatives.

On this visit, she stayed at Adam Reznicsek's home. Later, she married Adam's son, Joe. She had always loved to ride horses and rode well, so Dad saddled up George and asked Gladys not to run the horse because George couldn't use his hind legs properly. The idea was that I would ride bareback behind the saddle to the Reznicseks' house, then return home with George. I did all right until we finally got out to the main road. Gladys was so used to riding that the temptation was too great for her to bear, so she started running the horse. Since he didn't handle his rear legs too well, every time he used them, he would jar me. I kept slipping backwards and thought for sure I would fall off that plug. Anyway, we made it to the Reznicseks'. Then I rode George peacefully, as far as that was possible, back to our house.

Another time, Dad traded horses with someone while

we were driving teams hauling wood out of the timber and had a three-horse evener—a wagon made to haul four-foot pieces of wood. To hold the wood, the wagon had a Y-shaped (when viewed from the rear) iron framework that protruded over the wagon wheels. This framework's eight iron bars bent diagonally outward at the top. Horizontal bars bolted these pieces at the top to those before and behind them—four irons on each side. Then, the front and rear pairs of Y-shaped bars were chained together to keep them from spreading. The middle pairs of Y-shaped bars were not chained unless the load was unusually heavy. After we loaded the wood, it piled quite high above the ground level. The wagon tongue and two horses were on the other, all three pulling their share of a heavy load. While driving the wagon, the driver would sit on top of the wood on a gunny sack filled with straw.

After we had delivered the wood and Dad was coming home empty, he met a man walking through the timber from another road south of us, coming to visit Dad. When this man raised his umbrella, the new horse Dad had just traded for took off, and when it started going, the other two horses did also. The runaways ran through a gate, knocked it down, did some more damage, and roughed up the man who had raised the umbrella. Dad finally got them under control.

I remember another horse Dad acquired after I was out of school. Daisy was a mean character and wouldn't go through the rows as she should with the manually-operated cultivator, so when I tried to straighten her out, she became very agitated with me. She raised up on her hind legs and pawed at me with her front feet. I had to hold her bridle, and finally she calmed down.

World War I affected our family: Sherman had already joined the navy, and Weston had become a sharpshooter in the army. Now Oscar was drafted into the service and went to Camp Lewis in Washington State. All of the few from our Pentecostal group (to which Sherman and Weston did not belong) were conscientious objectors. They would do all they could as well as they could for their country as long as they did not bear arms with intent to take life. Some of their superior officers harassed them a great deal. One officer gave them all the dirty work to do— cleaning latrines, peeling potatoes, whatever. One time they asked Oscar whether or not he would give up his religion and take firearms with intent to kill. He refused, so they threatened him by putting a rope around his neck and pretending they were going to drown him in a barrel of water. I don't understand it all, but they were very hateful and unconcerned. Obviously, conscientious objectors did not enjoy a favored position.

One time in an open-air meeting in Portland while Oscar was based in Camp Lewis, God's presence came on him. With tears in his eyes he witnessed and testified in the street service. Conviction prevailed. He had endured some terrific persecution.

During World War I days and still before we had a car, Dad and Mother once wanted to attend a meeting held by the Trotter brothers in Mt. Scott, Portland. Mother wanted to take one of the young ladies from our community. Dad still had not received the Holy Spirit.

We went in a covered wagon with a horse team. The first night out, we camped not too far from a town with the Willamette Valley railway quite close by. (The logging companies' spurs branched off this one main line.) The train was packed with soldiers, whom we watched as the train went on its way either to camp or from one camp to another, we knew not where. Then we traveled on to the camp meeting in Portland.

Dad had watched Mother's life, and now he prayed and waited on the Lord, but when the last night came he still had not received the Spirit. During that last meeting, a lady came in, screamed, threw herself around, whipped her handkerchief back and forth, and made quite a commotion. Apparently, some demon power possessed her. Anyway, she distracted the service very much. When it was over we left and wended our way in the wagon back to our North Howell home. Dad still had not received the Spirit.

Later, some brethren came from Portland to the Reznicsek home. I don't remember the actual sequence of events that transpired, but they held a tent meeting that Dad attended. One of these preachers went into the audience after they had invited people to come, to repent of their sins, and to tarry for the infilling of the Holy Spirit. This man knew that my father had sought the Holy Spirit baptism off and on, so he went up to Dad and asked him if he was interested. While Dad tried to think of some way to answer the question to satisfy this preacher and yet leave himself in the clear, the preacher commented, "If you don't mean business, there's no use to fool with you." Then he left and walked on to talk to someone else. That gave Dad ample room to think and to consider that if he didn't mean business, it was true that the man didn't need to waste time on him as an individual. All this tended to make my father desire more to be filled with the Holy Ghost.

Time went on. Later on, in Brother and Sister Schmidt's home, Dad attended a night meeting. He'd become so hungry for the baptism of the Holy Ghost that he'd made up his mind to seek the Lord until he received Him. In a very unusual meeting in that country home that night, the preacher kept preaching away. He was doing a very good job, too, except that his shoestring kept coming untied. This preacher raised his foot up on a chair and commented that maybe the devil was having something to do with his shoestring coming untied all the time. One might not feel that in this atmosphere much spirit of conviction would prevail, but Dad was hungry. As a result, the Lord really gripped Dad's heart, touched his life and filled him with the Holy Ghost. Of course, through the years Dad had his struggles overcoming some of the things that the flesh is heir to, and these victories took time, but the Lord was gracious, and ultimately Dad died in the faith. Those were some of the early days prior to our knowledge of fuller truth that later on my father and mother embraced.

Those were called Council days. The Council later became known as the Assemblies of God. Although the people did not know about baptism in Jesus' name, the Spirit was present.

While we lived in North Howell and before the Christian and Missionary Alliance (CMA) came in, we attended the small trinitarian Pentecostal church. During this time, Dr. King, a member of our community, became irritated by our group of Pentecostals. One night a group of his friends gathered together and he beat up a preacher, Brother Barry, until the preacher's face was like beef pulp. This incident ended in a court case in Salem. Other men had made many threats before this. Persecutions changed from one type to another, but in the midst of it all, the Lord's name was magnified and glorified.

Brother Barry prayed for my father's mother, and God healed her of a fever. Years later, when she was at death's door and Dr. King went out in the countryside to see her, the doctor told her he didn't understand something. "With this sickness, you should have a fever." In her quiet, unassuming way, she told Dr. King that she had experienced something when Reverend Barry prayed for her (though she never became Pentecostal and still clung to her Baptist teaching, her chewing tobacco, and her corncob pipe), and she never had fevers as she used to before. Through the prayer of the man Dr. King had beaten, God had undertaken for her, and that's why she didn't have the fever Dr. King had said she should. Many things happen through the years to remind us that God is good to His church, His people, and His children and that we must respond to God's blessing in our lives.

One day while my brother and I broke up earth clods in a garden behind my uncle's back yard, and I worked ahead of Ray, who had a hoe and a hoelike instrument with three prongs instead of a blade, I don't know exactly what happened—either I stepped backward or Ray stepped too far forward, because one of these prongs entered my hip. It bled profusely.

The family hitched up the wagon to the horses and took me to a doctor in Silverton. He examined the wound, decided he wouldn't use any anesthetic, and started working. I toughed it out, he stitched it up, and everyone complimented me for being strong about it.

Near the end of the war, a black lady called Mother Brittain was either staying in our home or spending the day there (I don't remember which) and holding meetings in the area. Even though our area could sometimes get quite rough, God had used her a great deal. For example, Swede Johnson, who'd been a logger, was now under tremendous conviction.

This day, Dad planned to take a team of horses with a load of potatoes to Silverton. I went into the house to tell my mother good-bye because I was going with Dad. After I kissed Mother good-bye, Mother Brittain, standing by one of the windows, said, "Honey, ain't y'all goin' to kiss me?" What was I to do? I did, and then I went on my way. The Lord used Mother Brittain in those days. She had some good meetings in our community, after which she went to Portland.

Just before Dad and I left, we heard quite a noise emanating for six miles clear out to where we lived. As we neared town, the hullabaloo increased. It turned out to be a celebration for the first false armistice at the end of World War I. The townspeople had an effigy of the kaiser.

When the war did end, the Howard brothers came home, first Sherman and Weston. I still have a coin Sherman gave me from his days in the navy. Then they went to Idaho to homestead.

After Oscar's discharge, and while he contemplated whether or not to join his brothers in Idaho, some of our old friends, the Olsens, held special tent meetings in Silverton featuring Sister Hanks, who called herself a "mother in Israel." She had aspirations and felt that the Lord wanted her to marry my cousin Oscar Howard, who was many years younger than she. Oscar said to my dad, "Uncle John, I believe if God wanted me to marry her, the Lord could speak to me as well."

44

Oscar then asked Dad whether he should join his brothers in Idaho. Dad advised him not to go, setting forth his several reasons. For one thing, neither of his brothers were making any strong effort to serve God. However, Oscar had made up his mind to go, so he went.

There he came in contact with the Mormons (who saturated his community), accepted their teaching, and joined them. So did Sherman. Weston didn't concern himself too much with religion. Through the years, we have kept in touch. I saw Oscar in later years, a very staunch member of the Mormon Church. He died in that faith. In the midst of all this, we saw how God deals with humanity, working with individuals, trying to bring them to knowledge of Himself. Though in some cases people lost out and failed, yet God didn't fail—only the human element with which we all must deal.

The log cabin. Note the part of the roof on the end which the tree fell against many years previous to this that we never repaired.

Miss Rouse, Ellis Scism's first schoolteacher, going out for a picnic.

45

We knew how to use these apparently prehistoric tools in the lumber business, but since they have presently grown more obscure, I here explain three of the lesser-known ones:

1. This is a *footedge*. Because its designer apparently conceived of it primarily for human injury, we called it "shin hoe."
2. This is a *froe*. With this and other tools my father made the shakes for our log cabin roof.
3. This is a *peavy*. We would use these while dealing with logs. The hook swings in and out so that we could drag some logs in while pushing others away.

CHAPTER THREE

A New Beginning

On March 17, 1919, the Lord filled me with the Holy Spirit. Different homes in our community had held meetings. An elderly German man, Bill Sann, and his large Irish wife, neither of whom had received the Holy Spirit or even made a profession of faith, wanted to hold a Pentecostal service in their home as a community service. They invited us.

That night, the Spirit's power "slew" several people, including me. As I lay on the floor, the Lord began to speak through me in other tongues and I came to know the Lord in a new and definite way. Subsequent to this, I was baptized in Pudding River with the words "in the name of the Father and of the Son and of the Holy Ghost" said over me, but my initial experience was receiving the Holy Ghost, speaking in other tongues as the Lord's Spirit gave utterance. Mr. Sann said, "Ah-bah" (a broken Anglo-

Germanic expression), and added that I was too small to mimic God's move. He recognized my experience as God's work in my life.

After I received the Holy Spirit, several preachers from Oregon City came to our log house. Ralph Bullock came from Andrew C. Baker's church in Oregon City, and through his ministry, our community first heard about the oneness of God in Christ and baptism in Jesus' name, a wonderful message that we have since loved and appreciated so deeply. Ralph Bullock's ministry, as well as those of John Greene, Fred Jubb, Arthur Hodges, and some others of that era, impressed my parents very, very much.

Mother told us that one time as she prayed, she felt the Lord tell her to read the Book of Acts. She read it, and through God's Word received a revelation of the message of Jesus Name baptism. This stuck with her and ultimately caused her and Dad to go to Oregon City to be baptized by Andrew C. Baker in Jesus' name for the remission of sins. This happened soon after Brother Bullock's arrival in our house.

A few years later while we lived in Silverton, my brother, Ray, accepted Jesus Name baptism. Being younger, of course, I did not yet fully understand, but later on I saw the light and was baptized in Jesus' name for the remission of sins, also by Brother Baker.

Meanwhile, because we had accepted the truth, we had quite a difficult time until eventually we could no longer maintain the status of fellowship we had known. Finally, division came because Dad and Mother were baptized in the name of the Lord Jesus Christ. One night, one of the community home meetings called my parents to bring them to account. They had refuted the trinity doctrine but had not felt they should refrain from worshiping with trinitarians—they had no other place to worship.

However, after the community meeting called them into question concerning their stand for God's oneness, the people asked them to leave the meeting. One of the neighborhood ladies commented that when Brother and Sister Scism left the room to go home, she felt God's presence leave. This did not exclude us from all meetings in the area, only from those held by people who adhered to this particular decision.

When I was about fifteen, I saw the truth of baptism in Jesus' name and walked in it as my parents did. In retrospect, I thank God for His guiding hand and direction.

We still lived at the log house on a very muddy road when Dad purchased his first car: a brand-new 1927 Model T touring car with no battery. We started it by cranking it. We had our problems jacking it up, but if we got at least one rear wheel up, we could crank and start it more easily.

This car had a magneto, from which we got our lights. If we revved up the motor, the lights would shine somewhat brightly, but if we were slowing down trying to go through a gate, for example, the lights would shine very dimly. This was a source of irritation, but since we were poor and didn't have much, we were thankful.

We pay tribute to Henry Ford because cars cost so much less then than they do now (though we had less, of course). We were mighty, mighty happy to have a car to get around in.

Sometimes winters got so cold that we'd pour hot water in the radiator to warm up the motor. A lot of effort went into trying to keep Model T in good shape and running order.

Since the trinitarian church had now expelled us, we wanted to attend a Oneness church if possible, but the closest was far away in Oregon City. During the winter when mud made the side road impassable, we would keep our car at Uncle Bob's place and drive our team and sled to his house. Mother would put a lantern under the lap robes in the sled to keep us warm. We'd tie up the horses in Uncle Bob's shed, then drive into Salem, where Reverend Hansen led the Assemblies of God church and once invited me to speak, or to Silverton, which was closer and where the trinitarian church also gave us fellowship. Then we'd come home, hook up the team of horses again to the sled, put the car in the shed, and slide back to the log house where we lived.

Even at this early juncture, I can remember my mother sitting on the altar bench in Salem laughing with a holy laughter under the Holy Spirit's anointing.

Meanwhile, work on the land continued. Our surface well had hard water, and Mother could not adjust to it. Since Uncle Bob Scism had a well of soft water, my duties included, when I was about twelve, riding on a horse to his house and taking home a couple of jugs of water. After filling these, I'd wrap them in burlap and hang one on each side of the saddle. One time I tried to get up a little too much speed, and forgot about those jugs. The result was that as the jugs bounced back and forth one of them broke. That scared the horse. Then I had to do my first works over again.

Dad had rented some grazing land to Bill Sann, who one day came and announced that he wanted his calf out so he could take it with him. I told him I would go down in the pasture, get it, and run it up toward him. I jumped bareback on the horse, grabbed a strip of canvas to scare the calf with, and galloped off. I thought I would scare the calf back the other direction, but since the bridle had no blinders, the canvas scared the horse. The horse made an abrupt turn and I didn't. I just flew off and landed on my chest. This knocked the wind out of me and I took some time to recover.

As my brother and I grew, we learned the value of money and of work. We decided we needed a bicycle. Of course, we couldn't use it in the winter on the very muddy roads, but we sure would enjoy it in spring, summer, and autumn. Dad said that we could get one, but that we would have to cut some tree limbs. A man named Leslie would haul the limbs and sell them. We cut a lot of big limbs off some old fir trees and piled them up. Leslie came out, loaded up his truck, and sold the load. After deducting his expenses, he gave Dad the money and Dad bought the bicycle we wanted. We used it for a long, long time.

Another time, we wanted to get a twenty-gauge shotgun. Dad didn't mind, but of course we again had to work for the money. Mrs. Pottoff, a neighbor lady across the creek from us quite some distance away who had a lot of acreage on another road, said that we could hoe her corn. We hoed her corn and bought the gun. I left it with my brother, Ray, when my family went to India. In the early 1980s, he gave it to Harry, my son. We used the gun to shoot birds and rabbits. Our woods had a lot of cottontails.

The day came when we finally moved from the log cabin to Silverton to take care of my mother's father and mother, Frank and Mary Webb. Grandma and Grandpa

Webb's health had been going down for several years. Grandma Webb had experienced a bad stroke and wasn't well at all, and Grandpa Webb had cancer. This meant a lot of work for my mother. Dad would need to get a new job, and Ray and I would attend a new school. I had just turned twelve.

A Jesus Name meeting at the Scism log cabin sometime in 1918-21.

Ellis Scism on the left in fifth grade at North Howell school (1920-21)

CHAPTER FOUR

Silverton

*W*e moved to Silverton, a sawmill town, and Dad found work at Silver Falls Lumber Company Mills. The school there differed altogether from the old one in the country. The lower grades were nearer the high school and quite near the Christian church at that time.

Not too long after I joined the school in Silverton to begin sixth grade, the school began preparing for the Oregon State physiology exam. In North Howell, I had taken this and passed it, so I did not need to study it again. For some reason, students in Silverton had not yet taken this test and were still studying for it. When the teacher told them to get out their physiology books and open them to such and such a page, I opened my geography book. As the teacher walked down between the rows of students, observing the books they had opened on their desks, she came by my desk and saw that I was not studying the subject she had said we should. She reached down, picked up the physiology book, opened it to the page she had told us to study, closed the other book, and placed both in front of me. Very timid, docile, and withdrawn, I didn't say anything, just very meekly looked at the physiology book. She walked to the front of the classroom.

Then one of the girls spoke up in my defense and explained that I had already taken that subject in the school I'd come from and had passed the exam, so I didn't need to study it. The teacher came back to my desk, closed my physiology book, opened my geography book to where I had opened before, and placed both in front of me. Thus was I redeemed from her displeasure. I studied geography. I was amused and yet also half scared to death by it all.

Another time, this same teacher asked the class a question. I had never habitually raised my hand and snapped my fingers, so I don't know what came over me, but this time I thought I knew the answer, so without thinking I raised my hand and gave my fingers a snap. She looked at me and said, "Ellis, I'm no dog. You don't have to snap your fingers at me." That really put me in my place, and as you can see, I have not forgotten it.

At that school, the students could change rooms, so we had several teachers. On Washington's birthday my first year there, I thought I should get my teachers a card with a picture of Washington on it, or whatever I could find, as an expression of appreciation. The shop didn't have much of a choice of cards with different pictures or statements or poems on them. I bought three or four, one for each teacher, and handed the cards to them as I went to school. Then later I saw the teachers comparing their cards, and I felt embarrassed because my cards were mostly the same. I do not know just how they looked at it, but I was sorry I had not gotten cards far enough in advance to have each one different rather than them being similar.

In my last year in that school—eighth grade—one of our subjects was shop (wood working), which I'd be able to use later.

While we lived in Silverton, Sister Bates, a black preacher, would sometimes visit us. She and her husband, a well-known gambler who worked at one of the Salem hotels as a porter, didn't get along too well. I do not know the end of their life, but we became somewhat familiar with a part of it since she would come over to our place to get away from him.

One time she voiced the fear that he would come to our house to look her up, so Dad asked me to watch the bridge across the creek from where we lived on one of the main streets in Silverton. I knew where the bus would stop and what Mr. Bates looked like. The idea was to find out whether or not he had come on that bus, then report back home. The bridge wasn't far, so I took the old bicycle and rode over there. Sure enough, Mr. Bates stepped off the bus. I jumped on the bicycle and rode back across the bridge and to the house to let my parents know that Mr. Bates had arrived. I don't know the outcome, but I assume things worked out.

One time at the state fair in Salem, Mr. Bates was in a big crowd when some young white lady came along, took him by the arm, and said, "I caught a coon! I caught a coon!" Mr. Bates said, "Yes'm, and you didn't have to have an old dog to catch him either." Her tasteless humor back-fired: she'd tried to get him upset, but he hadn't, so she just ended up looking silly. He later said of this incident, "She beat herself so bad." He had quite a sense of humor.

Along with Mr. Bates's gambling instincts and his humor, he also had consideration for others in a less fortunate position than he. I remember him telling my parents that a drummer (traveling salesman with wares in a big trunk) used to come to Salem from Portland. Mr. Bates knew that the man's wife and children were in very dire circumstances because the drummer would spend his money on gambling and leave the family rather destitute. Mr. Bates knew the man's address, so when he won money off him, he sent it to the man's wife. Later, she traveled to Salem to see what kind of person this Mr. Bates was. She found to her astonishment that he was black. Mr. Bates could be rather oppressive and very difficult at times, especially to his wife, but underneath it all he did have some consideration for others.

While we lived in Silverton, we attended a lot of meetings. First, we went to a Pentecostal service in a little upstairs mission hall just across from the post. I was the janitor for this small congregation of mostly elderly people. We sometimes held outdoor meetings. I don't remember if this church declined, but later we attended the Christian Missionary Alliance (CMA) after they came and built a wooden building. They had many young people, and this naturally appealed to me as a young person.

When we first went to these meetings, they caused quite a discussion by some citizens of the community, who accused Dr. Betts, the speaker, of pushing people over and then claiming they'd been "slain" in the Spirit. He had practiced medicine somewhere back East and had linked up with the CMA. God used him a great deal in those days in healing ministry, and he had far-reaching results. Although people made many comments of one kind and another, some not so kind, he went on doing what he could in God's work in the light of what he understood to be God's plan and purpose.

After he left, Reverend Parrott came to Silverton. During his pastorate, some of us younger fellows in the church had an all-night prayer meeting. God began to deal with us through His Word and through the operation of His Spirit.

Meanwhile, I began working part-time at a grocery store operated by Brother Stenberg of the CMA congregation. He and his wife later began leading the Silverton CMA work, but Brother Stenberg, due to being a local businessman, hesitated to participate in the CMA open-air meetings. His wife became the main speaker and preacher of the work there after the other evangelists had come and gone.

Brother Stenberg and his wife felt that God had been dealing with my young heart, and they wanted me to go to the CMA Bible school in Seattle. That did not work out because I had already come in contact with Oneness Pentecostal truth and was standing for that even though Silverton had no church of our faith then.

Soon we could travel to church more easily. We'd had the car with the magneto. Eventually, things worked out more favorably and we got a car with a battery; the better lights made traveling much more pleasurable. A few days after buying this car, Dad lost control of it, drove it down in the ditch, kept going, and drove it back up on the road. We got along but did have a little excitement before it was over.

During this time, since we had no church of our faith in

Silverton, we kept contact with the Jesus Name people and churches in Oregon City, Independence, and Salem. Since Oregon City was about forty miles (maybe an hour and a half) away, we would usually drive twenty-one miles from Silverton to Independence and spend a Sunday there. By this time, Ralph Bullock, who had been Andrew C. Baker's assistant in Oregon City, where Brother Baker called him "my walking Bible," started a work in Independence using tent meetings. Brother Bullock had already brought our family to the Name truth, which was what the Jesus Name message was commonly called in those days. His ministry continued to help me a great deal as a young boy of twelve on up.

As time went by, we would travel to Independence. My father and mother would drive over there to church, take a lunch, stay until after the night service, and then drive back to Silverton. It was not too far, yet for a Model T Ford it was far enough. While going there, we met Brother and Sister George Farrell, who came from California.

We also met a former missionary named M. K. Van Horn, whom we always called Daddy Van. He and his wife had worked in Egypt for many years. God had performed a wonderful miracle in her life and healed her of dropsy—the disease had visibly oozed out of her skin's pores.

When I was thirteen or fourteen, Joe Reznicsek married Gladys Neeley. We attended the wedding at Andrew C. Baker's church, the only well-established Name church in the area.

Joe and Gladys Reznicsek stayed with Brother and Sister Bullock in Independence at that time and invited me to spend a week with them. We had night services and all ate at one community table—the Reznicseks, Farrells,

Bullocks, and I. We had a great time together.

Later, Joe, who already felt a ministerial call, and Gladys, who could sing and play the guitar, traveled with Mattie Crawford, a well-known revival and camp meeting evangelist baptized in Jesus' name.

Grandpa Webb eventually passed away when I was about fourteen. After this, for a brief while I stayed with Uncle Albert and his family. One evening, Melvin, their boy about my age, and I stayed out late playing with a wagon and didn't get in when we should have. My uncle had come home and was quite perturbed with us for not being there. When we got in, Melvin's sister Muriel suggested that her brother and I get to bed really quickly before Uncle Albert put in an appearance. We hustled off to bed and feigned sleep, and as far as I know, nothing was ever said. But we had a few trepidations.

After my grandfather and then my grandmother died, we briefly lived in the house that had belonged to them. The house had a two-bedroom apartment with one bedroom on either side of the kitchen-living room. This, Grandma and Grandpa had previously rented out to schoolteachers in town. While we lived there, a man named Peter Dugan stayed with us briefly. I recall first hearing him preach in Oregon City at Brother Baker's church. He didn't look nice by any yardstick, but he played the violin very well. I saw him play songs while holding the violin upside down. And he could thump away on the piano. Brother Baker used to say that if he could play without people having to look at him, that wouldn't be quite so bad. At any rate, Peter was quite an individual.

Mother and Dad slept in one of the two bedrooms downstairs, and since the upstairs rooms weren't rented to anyone, Ray and I used them. Peter slept in the middle room. At this time, my brother, who wasn't living for the Lord, came in late. Ray knew that this visiting preacher-singer-musician-whatever was asleep, so he tried to feel his way along and reach his bedroom without disturbing him, but as Ray tried to wend his way in the dark to the bedroom, he bumped into Peter Dugan's bed. Peter rose up and scared him. Lo and behold, the next morning when we got up, Peter was gone. He had left town and never did come back. I don't know what happened; apparently Ray had scared him quite severely. We saw Peter Dugan later, but never in the city.

Grandma and Grandpa Webb's house was sold by their children, so we moved near the sawmill in Silverton, where Dad had a job. When we lived there, I was about fifteen years old.

While we lived near the sawmill, Ralph Bullock moved from Independence to Salem and started a work there in his own home, later renting an upstairs hall. At this time, an evangelist, Jimmy Tolan, and his wife, held meetings at this Name church in Salem, pastored by Ralph Bullock. Meantime, my mother became very ill. Brother Bullock brought Brother Tolan to pray for her, and the Lord healed her.

About this time, Joe Rezniczek was driving back from a house church meeting in Jefferson, Oregon, to Salem one night when he got too close to the edge of the road. He got the car stopped, but it turned over on its side and two people in the car died: a black sister and a Mr. Wilson. Mr. Wilson had never given his heart to the Lord, though his wife was a dear elderly lady in the Salem church. The black sister had just testified in that meeting that no matter what happened, she was ready to meet the Lord. The sun shines on the just and on the unjust, on the ready and on the unready. Both the black sister and Mr. Wilson went into eternity that night. Joe Reznicsek took the accident very much to heart and was not himself for a long, long time.

Dad was unhappy in the sawmill because he worked on the Green Chain, where a conveyer belt would carry in huge cantilevers quickly, one right after another, each one anywhere from four to ten inches square and four to twelve feet long. His job was to check and change these cantilevers to the appropriate conveyer belt to be carried to the saws. It was exhausting work.

Meanwhile, we moved to another house in Silverton. (I don't remember why.) Here I saw in a dream or vision many dark-skinned people going over an abyss. This was my first feeling for India. Of course, I knew the Reznicseks were planning to go there.

I was happy when Dad told the family that he had another job lined up and that we'd move to the country (though I did prefer the education at the town school). He quit work at the sawmill, and we moved to a hop ranch called the Benson place a few miles away.

We were living there when I graduated from the eighth grade in the Silverton school. Since we had moved to the Benson ranch, we had some distance to go to and from school. I could not afford books to go to high school, so I could do nothing but go to work. Through Dad I got a job clearing brush for someone not far from where we lived. I worked at that for some time, then at the Benson place.

Mr. Benson had a lot of hops. The hop season was always an interesting time of year. Dad and the other workers replaced rotten poles, attended to the wires

61

reaching from pole to pole, and attached the strings reaching from the hop vines to the wires. The vines would climb poles and strings up to the wires, making picking easier. Naturally, the workers also cultivated them for the good of the hops' growth. Finally, during picking season, the workers bickered in a friendly way during weighing. After that, they carefully watched the hop kilns to make sure the hops weren't discolored.

During this time, we attended church in Salem and again met Daddy Van, who subsequently spent many nights in our home on the Benson place. He seemed to take a liking to me and he'd sometimes visit the house for a weekend. Upstairs we had a big room with two double beds. Early in the morning he'd wake up, throw his pillow at us boys, and tell us it was time to get up.

I remember a footwashing service in Salem when we men sat across from each other and a basin was placed between each pair of men. While Daddy Van was having his feet washed, suddenly God's blessing hit him. His feet bounced up and down in the washbasin, and the water splashed all over where he was sitting. He was a very happy person.

Ralph Bullock moved out of the upstairs hall and into a storefront building on State and Commercial. The Lord blessed many hungry hearts in some wonderful meetings there. Brother and Sister Teffree came in special services before they went to India as missionaries. Later still, they returned to Norway, and I completely lost track of them. Sister Teffrey was the main speaker at their meetings. After visiting us, they were with Brother Opsand in Seattle.

Meanwhile, God kept dealing with me through Joe and Gladys Reznicsek relative to going to India as a missionary.

I looked up to Joe very much. He'd been my friend throughout boyhood, was thirteen years older than I, and left for India as a missionary around this time (1924) with Gladys and their baby son, Joseph Arthur. A lot of their support came from George Studd, a missions-minded layman. In those days, much emphasis was placed on faith missionary efforts, and there was much antipathy toward organized Pentecostal missionary endeavor.

Meanwhile, we moved from the Benson place back to the log house in North Howell. Gladys Reznicsek died at Bharosa Ghar Mission in North India, and Sister McCarty, the leader of the mission, brought Joseph Arthur back to the States as a toddler when she came by ship. Joe Jr. lived with his grandparents, while Joe Sr. stayed in India, bestowing affection on Indian children while tears ran down his face.

I remember Joe Sr.'s mother telling my mother one time, "Joseph is all right now." She had not understood why. Later she told her son about it, and he answered that at the very moment the Lord had spoken to her, he was being baptized in Jesus' name. Adam and his wife were very staunch trinitarians, and Joe's testimony didn't change that, though they treated Joe kindly.

When Sister McCarty went back to India at the end of her furlough, she took with her Emma Gillette, who in India became Joe's second wife. Soon after, Emma developed a dental problem and had to travel two miles from Bharosa Ghar to Turtipur Railway Station, then by train to Lucknow. On the way, during this season of the "loo" winds, Emma had a heat stroke through the ear and died after they reached Lucknow. We heard of all these events through letters that trickled in slowly over a period of years while I worked in the timber in North Howell.

I already had a call to India, and I knew about these things that had happened to Joe, but we felt that our consecration should be great enough to warrant taking a risk.

School in Silverton (1921-24). Ellis is third from the bottom on the right, wearing spectacles.

CHAPTER FIVE

Country Work

After moving from the Benson place back to North Howell, we continued our work in the woods. Before felling a tree, we'd always face the tree so we'd have some reasonable idea of where the tree would fall. A tree might look as if it would fall a certain direction, but many variables would influence the fall, so we'd face it. Facing the tree involved two men making a horizontal cut with a falling saw, followed by using an acute angle axe to cut down toward the falling saw cut. We'd do this on the side where we wanted the tree to fall. Then we would go around to the opposite side and start with our seven-foot falling saw, arcing around from the back side until the tree fell.

One time my father, brother, and I felled a very large red fir on our property. This tree was so large that we could not simply saw through it. Also, we ran into quite a seam of pitch. Knowing that this often happened while cutting down trees, we kept a bottle of kerosene handy to grease the saw to make it easier to pull through the pitch. We had to keep greasing the saw quite frequently depending on the amount of pitch that would collect on the saw itself. We also had to cross-section the saw because we could not just start and go through. Ultimately, we felled the tree.

When it fell, it embedded itself deeply in the earth. By that year, I was about the same height I am now (six feet, one inch), and the base of the tree was much higher than my head. That was a very large tree. I don't think I ever helped fell one any larger. We cut it up for firewood.

Our cutting up a seven-foot-diameter tree for firewood might horrify someone with modern ecological sensitivities, but in those days, timber covered the land everywhere for miles. And our timber work didn't ruin the land—it turned to productive use as farmland. If you follow Highway 99 from Salem to Oregon City, you see hop yards, berry farms, fruit orchards, and vegetable farms.

Sometimes when I helped my father, we worked trees on steep terrain. When we would face a tree one side of which was much lower than the other, we would have to make a springboard by nailing a horseshoe to the edge of a board six inches wide, two inches thick, and six to eight feet long. We'd make a cut in the tree and embed the board edge with the horseshoe into the cut. The ridge along the horseshoe toe would dig into the upper side of the cut and hold the board in place. One man would stand on the ground on the high side, and the other man would stand on this springboard as we did our felling, moving the springboard (by swiveling it in the existing cut or making a new cut) as occasion demanded.

After felling a tree, we would trim off all the limbs with an axe, then begin to cut the trunk. My dad had what we called a one-man saw—a gasoline-powered saw to cut a felled tree into sixteen-inch lengths. With dogs (long-handled metal hooks) we'd maneuver fallen trees into place to saw them. Dad had built a framework to secure the saws and keep them still while he filed them, so we didn't have to stand there and hold them for him. His filing tools were a spider (named for the shape), filers, a file set, and another tool the name of which I can't recall. The one-man saw would cut down through the wood pretty well on its own without our having to push it down, though we still had to keep individual teeth from dragging. After cutting the sixteen-inch wooden wheels from the trunk, we'd cut them like pies into wedges, using a sledgehammer and wedge.

Smaller trees we would cut into four-foot lengths using a crosscut saw that could have one or two handles, according to the width of the tree. My dad often accused me of riding the saw (not pulling my weight) and I suppose sometimes I unconsciously did, and I also didn't know how to crosscut well yet.

Before we had trucks of any kind, we used horses to haul loads from the timber. Sometimes, when the soil was soft, we would haul partial wagonloads to a decent road, then, when we took out our last partial load, top it off with the stock wood stored up earlier. We hauled heavy, heavy loads to Salem or sometimes to Mount Angel. In this way, along with farming and other versatile work, we earned our living on the ranch.

Uncle Bob had an old Model T Ford truck with an open bed, solid rubber tires on the rear, and pneumatic tires in the front. I first learned to drive on this thing at around sixteen years of age. My brother already knew how to drive, being four years older. Occasionally some boys would come out to our log house on the ranch and spend a weekend with us. Sometimes when I'd drive the truck, I'd zigzag down the road with boys sitting on the back end. Not having pneumatic tires on the rear helped create a bit of excitement when the pavement was wet. We had a lot of fun until we learned to do better.

This was only the beginning of sorrows. Now I wanted to buy a Model T Ford of my own. My uncle had an old 1924 touring-top car with side curtains. To buy this from him, I worked in the woods for Uncle Bob, cutting up trees that had been felled.

Uncle Bob had a gasoline-powered saw on runners and with a cable. After we'd trimmed a tree with axes, we'd pull this saw parallel to the log, dog the cable way up into the smaller part of the tree, and with another dog keep the saw's vibration from moving the saw away from the tree. Then we'd start the first sixteen-inch cut. After the saw completed that, I'd set it running on a new cut, and while it cut, I'd split the old cut with sledgehammer and wedge. If the tree had no sap and an even grain, I could dispense with the wedge and split the wood with the sharp end of the sledgehammer head. I would cut sometimes four cords of wood a day, sawn and split. It was work, but I was strong and healthy, so I enjoyed it. I used the gasoline-powered saw to cut the wood and my muscle to split the sixteen-inch cuts into pie-shaped firewood pieces. Fortunately, a tree cut in sixteen-inch blocks is easily split. That's how I earned the money to pay for this Model T.

Around this time, my brother, Ray, got married. After

he left school, he worked in the logging camps near Dallas, Oregon. There he fell on some logs and injured his back, so he came back and worked for different people in the Howell area. He married Maybelle McClellan. Her oldest sister had married Harry Judd, and they had three girls and eventually a son, Edwin. Ray, Maybelle, and I drove my car to an Assemblies of God youth rally on the coast, taking along a couple of young ladies from the Salem church.

Maybelle served the Lord and was spiritually minded; Ray did off and on, and he still had his temper. One day while Arthur Hodges and I picked strawberries at the Bensons' berry patch, some Italian berry pickers also picked away nearby. I heard one of these boys yell out that so-and-so was not strong, but just smelled like it. I liked that expression.

Time went by, and one day when Mother and Maybelle were outside a quarrel arose. (Ray was somewhat belligerent at times, so something would come up.) I called out to Ray, "You're not strong, you just smell like it." He was highly incensed, caught me under the clothesline, and began squeezing my throat. I thought he was going to choke the daylights out of his little brother. That caused quite a furor with Mother and Maybelle. They yelled at him to stop, so he simmered down and the dastardly deed was not committed, but he still did not feel too joyful about my remark. He left quite an imprint and an impression on me. I knew he was hot-tempered, so to just holler out something like that was not a very smart thing to do. Now, of course, years have come and gone and we get along much better, but in those days he was very quick-tempered.

On the other hand, Ray was very generous. We used to

say that Ray would get mad at the drop of a hat when someone would cross him. Yet, the next minute, he would turn around and give his shirt to someone, whereas his brother, namely one Ellis Scism, would not forgive so easily. He was classed as being somewhat stubborn, and the Bible says that's as bad as witchcraft. I would not forget things as soon as Ray would and had a tendency to hold a bit of a grudge.

My relationship with Dad was a little better, and we had some good times. Sometimes he would take a team of horses and the wagon to pick up timber or potatoes. I'd tease him and he'd tease me—both of us threatening to throw the other off the wagon. One time we picked up two young ladies in the wagon to give them a lift, then started acting drunk to scare the life out of them.

One time I went into the bedroom while Dad still slept, removed his covers, took him out of bed and onto the floor. But this was just fun—I never lost respect for him.

One time I came out of the house to see Dad sitting hunched over on the back porch, which was about six or seven feet wide and twenty feet long, down low to the ground. I came up behind Dad and gave him a push. He lost his balance and fell, and his nose dug a little furrow in the soil. He looked up and said, "Ohhh, Ellis." I hadn't meant to push that hard, and I felt bad about it.

Dad took a contract with the paper mill, cutting white fir. We had to trim the bark off these smaller trees with a tool that went around the trunk. If we peeled bark when the sap was high, we could clear it away from the wood easily. Then we'd split up the wood in four-foot lengths, again cut by the cord.

One time as we felled white fir in one area not too far

from our North Howell home, the wind blew over us and also over a tree that long ago had started to fall but had lodged into another and broken some limbs. That's when we most needed to watch and be careful. I trimmed a fallen tree nearby, my head bent over, leaning forward and trimming with the double-bitted axe. (We'd never heard of hardhats.) I heard a swish, and almost immediately something brushed down my back, then ran down into the ground behind me. A limb broken off long ago had, by reason of the blowing wind, fallen from the dead tree. Being a bent limb, it had just glanced off my back and down into the ground behind me. Had I been standing upright and not leaning forward, the limb would have hit me on the head, and who knows what might have happened? Working in the timber always involved danger.

Later, Dad bought a Model T Ford truck with pneumatic tires. It had a Ruxtell axle, not too common in those days but used occasionally to give one more power in the timber. Not too many Ruxtell-axled vehicles were on the road; it had more speed than most trucks. Sometimes we would use this truck to do odd jobs for neighbors.

For example, one time Dad asked me to take Pete Ditchen, a neighbor's son, to Mission Bottom, a Willamette River point several miles from where we lived, and bring back a load of gravel. I left our house, picked up Pete at his parents' house, and drove the truck.

As we drove down in the low-lying area by the river, suddenly something happened to the front wheel. When we checked, we found that a spindle going down through the axle had broken. We had to walk some distance to get a new spindle bolt. After I repaired it, we continued down and loaded up our gravel. Of course, in those days we

71

shoveled by hand—we had no fancy equipment such as graces our modern mechanized age. When we felt we had a heavy enough load, we started back to North Howell. By this time, our repair had made us very late, but at least we were on our way.

We reached the top of the incline out of the Mission Bottom area when suddenly a valve stem sheared off a rear tire and it went flat. The rear tires were much larger than the front ones—the front were just thirty by thirty by three and a half inches. The back ones were huge, and we could do nothing but drive the truck to a yard belonging to some people in that area, leave it there, and start walking home. Pete had boots on—not very comfortable to walk in because one's feet can become very hot—so every once in a while he'd see a puddle and walk through the water to cool off his feet. We had quite a long distance to go and it was night, so we kept on walking.

Since we had borrowed some tools from a service station where we had bought the spindle bolt for the front wheel, we had to take these tools back. I told Pete that, rather than making him walk to the station some distance from the road we were on, I would return the tools, and he could just wait at the road until I came back. He did.

My dad and mother had, in the meantime, become very concerned as to what had happened to Pete and me. Dad and Ray came looking for us, found us alongside the road walking toward our home several miles away and took us home. The next day, we repaired the tire, brought the load of gravel to Mr. Ditchen's home, and unloaded it.

In winter, this road, now called Scism Road, became very muddy. It had only two houses on it—ours and a little one not far away built by my uncle. Otherwise, we traveled quite a long distance through the wood to come out in the area called Central Howell.

One night out in the rain and mud with the Model T Ford truck, the forward band went out, so I had to use the reverse band to get back home. I don't know how many miles I had to go in reverse, but the deep ruts in the muddy road made staying on track and getting home much easier. When the weather got really bad, we went back to the sled and kept the car in Uncle Bob's shed for main road use.

Sometimes I had to go out to the gas barrel to siphon gas for the truck. One day, I needed to go to Hubbard, another little town, for my trumpet lessons. Mother would be going with me since we had a few miles to travel to meet the other band members. While siphoning the gas, I did not withdraw my mouth from the hose in time, so I swallowed a lot of gasoline. All the way to Hubbard and in my mother's discreet presence, I kept belching. It was not a very pleasant feeling.

Later, because we had a surface well with hard water in North Howell and Mother, whose health was frail, could not adjust to it, we had to leave the ranch. Dad obtained a job working for the Salem city sewer department.

We had attended church in Salem, hauled pulp wood and sixteen-inch firewood to Salem, and covered the fourteen miles with a horse team and heavy wood load in a full day—leaving in the early morning and arriving in late afternoon back home from Salem. Now we lived there. I didn't care about the move one way or the other—Mom's health came first.

John Scism and sons, Raymond and Ellis, in 1924, cutting timber. Ellis is 15.

Grace Scism and
Gladys Rezniscek

CHAPTER SIX

Salem

*I*n Salem, Dad worked for the city sewer department, which, in addition to maintaining the sewers, also put in street curbs and did other city work. During his years there, he had a lot of experiences, some very enjoyable and some not so. One time while digging a very deep sewer ditch, sliding pea gravel almost buried him—a very precarious situation.

Prior to this experience, he had a premonition in which he visualized a coffin, with himself in it, floating near him. Just afterward, the pea gravel caved in and almost buried him. Fortunately, others came to his rescue and brought him out. Though he didn't feel too good about the event, still, his life had been spared.

After I reached eighteen or nineteen years of age, I worked for a Salem cannery. So did Ray. I did a lot of odd jobs, but ultimately, because Andy, the syrup maker, became sick due to too much sugar in his system, I was asked to become the syrup maker.

I had this job upstairs. Many bins full of sugar sacks lay on either side of the corridor leading up. I mixed the ingredient percentages in the syrup depending on what fruit the cannery was running. For example, if they were running prunes, I'd reduce the sugar, since prunes take a lower percentage than some of the other fruits. I'd dump the sugar in the hopper, which would then run down through mixing-tank pipes under pressure and into one of the ten fifteen-hundred-gallon stainless steel gravity-fed mixing tanks in an adjoining room. When they needed a smaller run, I would mix the syrup in a smaller tank. A pump would then pump the syrup from the mixing tank up to the supply tank, from which the syrup would run down to the machines through which the cans ran.

One day, since I didn't think I had anything to do, I sat on some empty sugar sacks in my room, reading a book, maybe one of Zane Grey's novels. I happened to look down the long corridor and saw my boss coming. He came up to me and said, "Ellis, if I were you I would keep busy doing something. Try to show that you're taking care of things and so on." I heeded his advice. After all, there was something—in fact, plenty of things—to do.

After I had worked at the cannery hours and hours, I would go home and be dead to the world. One night my mother, and Andy with her, came upstairs while I slept to inform me that I had to go back that night for a night shift. We had a long, long siege.

At the cannery two boys came to work to help me. These chaps didn't have any good principles. For example, to keep the sugar from seeping out, the company used white sacks inside the big burlap sacks. When we put in a big supply of sugar, we might empty any number of sacks into the big mixing tank. These kids would make off with the white sacks. It was just plain stealing and I didn't like it, but they insisted on doing it and who was I other than just an employee along with them? Though I was supposed to straw-boss the job, I didn't want to squeal on them.

Another thing they did: while we ran peaches through, they would set a jar of peach juice by the mixing tank, which operated by steam and would get hot. After a while, the juice would become rather strong and the possibility arose of them becoming a little stewed themselves. I got tired of that after a while, and they didn't last long.

One night when I was off duty and had gone home, one of the head men called for me to come. The sugar had coagulated, crystallized, and filled up the pipes, so the pump wouldn't put it through. They concluded that the best way to melt the sugar was to turn on the steam hose. Then the sugar would liquefy and the pump would take off and pump it into the mixing tank. It was a very bright idea, of course, but they had forgotten one thing—the sprinkler systems would melt after they reached a certain temperature. The bosses and employees had steam all through that area of the cannery when suddenly the sprinklers cut loose and water sprinkled over everything. After all, they were there to keep the building from burning up. The water sprinkled and sprinkled and soaked the entire area to two inches' depth and in the bottom of each of the hundreds and hundreds of sugar sacks in these bins, two inches of sugar had crystallized. It was all hopeless for our purposes.

77

I worked there until canning season closed. A cannery still operates there, as far as I know.

During those days in Salem, we went to Brother Bullock's mission. While we worshiped at State and Commercial, one time he asked me to lead the songs during youth service. I declined because I was too bashful to stand up in front of everybody. Finally, I told them that I could announce the number if someone else could lead the song. One of the young ladies in the mission did, then she'd sit down and I'd pop up to announce the next song's number. Then I'd sit down and she'd stand up again and lead the next song.

Later, a problem arose there. My dad, a deacon in the church, and Brother Bullock did not see eye to eye. Brother Bullock had a very strong personality and so did Dad. It was a case of come out or come under. We came out. Dad stepped down from his position, and for several months we went to a trinitarian church, since the area had no other Oneness church. One time the trinitarian church wanted to appoint me as youth group secretary, but of course they had a ruling that one had to be a member of the church, so at one youth meeting they just passed a card in front of me and asked me to sign my name, but I wouldn't do it. That took care of that.

Another time, while a group of us sat in the choir on the platform and the pastor's wife led the testimony service, one of our Name brethren from Corvallis testified. He spoke about the goodness of the Lord, how Jesus becomes sweeter and sweeter, and how his cup was full and his saucer, too. He testified about how wonderful it was of the Lord to let us know Him, when the pastor's wife turned around and told us that he was "Jesus Only."

Though we may object to the pejorative terms others may use of us, yet when we begin to exalt the Lord and magnify His Name, before long others will become aware that we do love the Lord in an unusual and different manner from many of our contemporaries.

We went to that church until after Ralph Bullock left and took a church in Yakima, Washington. Then Brother and Sister Hurt came to Salem and held a tent meeting. We went to these meetings and began to work toward coming back to the Oneness church.

Brother Hurt greatly influenced my life, and I appreciated his ministry very much. He played the organ well, and their ministry blessed us, even though they stayed for only a short time. Then, Kenneth Wine and his wife came to Salem for about six months, during which they held meetings in the upstairs mission on State Street where Brother Bullock had moved the church from State and Commercial. Finally, Brother and Sister W. L. Stallones pastored the mission. We attended there all the time, as far as I recall, and I remember many of those early days in Salem with pleasure, knowing that God works all things out in honor of His name as we put our trust and confidence in Him and in His ability to guide and direct His church. The Salem church, though, had about forty-seven different pastors over time, and no real growth until Brother Albert Dillon came there.

I met Larry Nugent in Salem while he engaged in prison evangelism there—this was his burden throughout his ministry. He would visit churches, entering late with his briefcase in one hand and his topcoat over the other. One time he almost hung himself trying to demonstrate to a congregation how the state hung prisoners on death row.

I had a Model T with a touring body, but I wanted a different car body, so I bought a coupe body with a front bench seat. I thought the car needed more seating, so I made a rumble seat in back that two people, if they were not too large, could sit in. I don't recall just how well this was done, but it didn't leak water. It was quite an interesting Model T with an extra oil line. I appreciated it very much.

During the time, I visited Mulino, where Harry Judd and his family lived. Ray, who became their brother-in-law, introduced their five-year-old son, Edwin, who owned a popgun, to real guns. Edwin still remembers my black car with its orange stripe and rumble seat.

As time went by, the church in Salem changed. Brother Sanders and different ones came through, and in 1931 Brother Joseph Reznicsek returned from India. In the meantime, Brother and Sister A. O. Moore came through Salem and mentioned an opening at the big downtown mission in Oakland, California. Having a call to missions work in India and a desire to work for the Lord, and having manifested that desire (though I was somewhat timid in testifying as I should, I did have a yearning and hunger to do something in Master's harvest field), I took the opportunity and agreed to go to Oakland.

Emmanuel Full Gospel Church, the Jesus Name church on 17 Chemmel St. in Salem.

Daddy Van and Ellis Scism (age 17) in 1926.

Ellis Scism on the mandolin.

81

Ray and Ellis Scism

Ellis Scism with a
moustache

82

CHAPTER SEVEN

Joining the Mission Home

I knew nothing about Bible colleges and would not, for lack of finance, have been able to go to a regular one if we'd had any modern ones in those ancient days. However, through Brother and Sister A. O. Moore I first learned about the possibility of going to the Harry and Maudie Morse Mission Home on 62nd Avenue in Oakland, California, to be trained at the mission on Ninth Street. Brother and Sister Morse allowed only two or three young men in the home at a time, so I felt really fortunate to be admitted there.

Through correspondence the opening came for me to go by faith and trust the Lord to see me through, which He did. Students entered the home as workers for the Lord and trusted Him for whatever He would provide. At the mission home, we would have no fees, but very little income either. Since I had almost no money, I very definitely had to trust God.

In May, Joseph Reznicsek and I started driving to Oakland, California—he on furlough and me to study in the big, old downtown Ninth Street Mission.

Our trip down to Oakland was interesting. We had eleven flat tires on the same wheel between Salem and Oakland. Thus California greeted me. Of course, travel in those days differed so much from today; we didn't have the nice freeways, so the journey took three or four days.

Our first night out we spent in Creswell, Oregon, with Brother Reznicsek's second wife's parents (his first two wives had passed away in India)—Professor and Mrs. Gillette. That night as we endeavored to sleep or perhaps had gone to sleep, the old-fashioned iron springs suddenly slipped down through the frame on Brother Reznicsek's side and crashed on the floor. We lay there laughing while Daddy Gillette came upstairs in his union suit and wanted to know what in the world had happened. My side of the springs was all right, but on the low side, where Joe had been sleeping, repairs were effected, and ultimately we had a good night's sleep. The next day we departed to continue our way to Oakland.

At that time, Ferne Gleason, Rose Ibe, and others worked at a woolen mill in Eureka, California. We spent one night there on the way.

Joe had packed a lot of things from India. At the California border, we had to lay everything out on a bench. These souvenirs—a little carved scorpion, things in formaldehyde, and so on—intrigued the border agent.

We went on into California, and I entered Ninth Street Mission Home. During those first days, second thoughts entered my mind. I missed Mother and Dad from Salem, but I felt God had guided me to Oakland and wanted me there because, long before this, I had felt the Lord speaking to me about India, and Ninth Street Mission Home was classified as a missionary home. Also, I knew quite a number who had gone to the Ninth Street home years before, so I looked forward to the experiences I would obtain while there.

In the home, workers did what they could to help. I worked quite a lot washing dishes and in the yard. Joseph Marata, a Japanese who preceded me as gardener, did a beautiful job and had everything looking great.

Not every event went smoothly. For example, one time, although I was supposed to have about two shirts in the wash each week, behold, things got out of hand and I had about eight shirts in the wash. The ladies in the home rotated ironing duties. This day, Brother Morse asked Ruby Martin, his secretary, to come down to the office at the mission on Ninth Street to do typing or shorthand. She mentioned having some ironing to do. He wanted to know more particulars. She told him she had about eight shirts of mine to be ironed. As a result, Sister Morse laid it on rather heavily at our evening meal, scolding me in no uncertain way in front of everyone. The combined guilt and shame overcame me, and I cried as I washed the dishes that night. From then on, I tried to watch things very carefully. We learned along the way as time went by.

I slept in a canvassed-off area in the garage. My place had its own raised wooden floor covered with carpet and a chest of drawers. It wasn't fashionable, but when someone went to the home, he got what he could—and it was nice.

My Model T helped the mission home in many ways, being more economical than the mission home car—an old

85

Velie touring car in which the workers rode to and from Ninth Street Mission and the home. Some months after I arrived, they replaced the Velie with a Packard.

Once I backed some of the cars out of the garage and parked them in front of Brother and Sister Morse's home. I put out the Packard and the Morses' Willys Knight (a four-door, silent-motored car). The garage had room for three cars, one in front of the other on the left and the third car on the right. We had to park one in the street in order to get the back one out of the garage. Since the Model T had gone in last at night, naturally it came out first in the morning. This day, I parked it out front and went about my day's duties. Later, I looked out and the Model T was gone, stolen, purloined, thieved, pinched. I had no idea who had taken it.

We reported it to the police, who later informed us that they'd found it not too far from the home, in East Oakland. We went there and, sure enough, found it, but whoever had stolen the car had jacked it up under the oil pan and stolen the speedometer cable and the Model T's one and only front spring. To keep the car from rolling down the hill they had placed another jack in front of one rear wheel. (I had more jacks after that theft.) We actually lost only the speedometer cable and the front spring. Before we could move the car, of course we had to buy a used front spring and install it. Fortunately, springs didn't cost much in those days. We never did anything about the speedometer cable; thereafter I guessed my speed from the engine noise. The hilarious thing is that the two jacks left had more value than the spring did, so we came out all right on the deal. I had the Model T for a long time and drove it to Clear Lake Oaks for Marj's and my honeymoon.

The home contained many mission people, such as Aunt Maudie (Sister Morse's aunt). This rather heavyset, tall lady lived in a little cabin near the large house where Thompsee resided. She always had her meals with the rest of us in the home, along with, sometimes, Thompsee. One time Aunt Maudie accidentally sat on the glass pane I had cut for a window and had temporarily laid on the bed before installing. Of course, once she'd sat on it, I couldn't really install it. We called her cabin the Sheep Shed because periodically church workers' babies were born there—occasions usually presided over by Dr. Dobson, a great friend of the Morses.

Thompsee was Sister Thompson, a retired school-teacher who had once owned the home and, about to lose the property, had deeded it over to Brother and Sister Morse on the condition that she could stay there as long as she lived, which she did. Very often she would cook for herself, and at other times she ate with the rest of us at the long dining room table. There a good number would come for prayer and for the Bible studies that Brother Morse or whoever was helping him would have. Sometimes they would come for meals, but not often.

Thompsee loved cats, especially one called Beauty, for whom she would often leave something in the refrigerator in the home, together with a little piece of paper on it indicating that this was for Beauty. This kind act of leaving meat we mission home students appreciated. We would so often hunger for meat. One time we came home to find some very fine meat purchased for Beauty. We were so overcome with hunger that we ate some of Beauty's meat. We didn't do it again, but we enjoyed it while we were at it.

When I first went down, Eva Wagner was the head worker in the mission home. Now she lives in Turlock and we have not heard too much of her over the years. She greatly helped and encouraged me. After Eva Wagner left, Flossie Seagraves, a registered nurse from St. Louis, succeeded her as Brother Morse's main worker. She took a strong lead in helping in the work there in the home and at the mission.

One night while Flossie drove to the mission and I sat on one of the jump seats in that old seven-passenger vehicle (or eight passengers, or maybe nine, determined by the size of occupants), I engaged in my habit of comparing California's climate with Oregon's. I did this without meaning harm or disrespect to anyone, but apparently I rode it rather heavily. That evening Flossie responded to my cogent comment about the weather by telling me that if I liked the climate so much better in Oregon, why didn't I go back? That really brought me to a halt because I hadn't come to Oakland with any intention of leaving until the proper time. After that, I kept my mouth shut concerning the relative climates of Oregon and California.

Flossie's sister, Faith, also stayed at the home. Although not a registered nurse like her sister, she had some practical nursing. Not too long after Joe and I got to Oakland, he and Faith Seagraves were married in the mission home. I stood up with Joe for the occasion.

Joe bought an old Dodge car in California. Two years later, over a two-month period I traveled nine thousand miles in this car with him, with Faith, and with my bride.

Some time after I came, Allan Burgess and his wife, Hazel, came to work in the home. The home had no electric dishwasher, so, to a great extent, I washed the dishes, pots, and pans, and Brother Allan dried them, or sometimes vice versa. We could always tell by whoever was going to do the cooking how much washing we'd have. We would put the pots and pans in their proper places, but the lids we'd give a toss and let them land where they would in one of the cabinets under the sink. We kept that door closed.

One day when Flossie came to cook, Brother Burgess and I were in the dining room next to the kitchen and heard her heels clicking as she walked down the hallway. She sailed into the kitchen and opened the cabinet door, and we heard those lids slide out on the floor. Brother Burgess and I decided the best thing we could do was take our exit, so we slipped down the stairway. Two doors led into the kitchen—one from the hallway and the other from the dining room. Down the hallway we sped and out of the way. We had a lot of laughs over that experience, especially since it dealt with an individual who was a bit short on being good-natured and taking things in stride.

James Marata, who preceded me as gardener at the home, left the mission home not long after I arrived. He was Japanese and had lived in Los Angeles and attended the Foursquare Bible school (Aimee Semple McPherson's). After he received the light on baptism in Jesus' name and Brother Morse baptized him, he stayed in the mission home for a while and later felt a call to go back to Japan as a gospel worker among his own people. Before he left, he gave me a Jamieson-Fausset-Brown commentary that I later took to India, had rebound there, and still keep in Brother Marata's memory. He wrote me a letter after reaching Japan and told me that he missed my Abrahamic hands. I used to sit about the middle of the dining table, so I would pass whatever was needed on my right or left. He remembered my long fingers, which he called Abrahamic.

When we went to India in 1949, we tried to look him up, but didn't have a clue where he was. We met an American colonel who knew all the ministers and chaplains but couldn't locate Brother Marata at all. Later on, we heard that he had been in Taiwan during those days, then had come back to Japan and had an orphanage there—had done a great work for the Lord. On our way from India in 1962, we saw him at the Japanese conference at Chigosaki when we stayed for a week or so with Brother and Sister Hubert Parks and dedicated the Parkses' boy. Seeing him was so pleasant after all the years we had been separated.

Days come and go, but God remains faithful to all who trust and confide in Him and in His ability to guide and to direct His church.

Lee Nugent stayed briefly in the home after his wife died. I've thought a lot of this very fine brother with whom I worked in Ninth Street.

Lee's son, Joseph, people called Junior. One day this little fellow sat on the back porch singing about climbing Jacob's ladder—"Each step brings us one round higher." I looked down at him and asked, "Junior, how long will you take to reach the top if you go one round a day?" He squinted up at me and said, "I'm just singing." So often in churches even today people just do a lot of singing. (Of course, the songs have undergone a drastic change from when I was a young whippersnapper.)

Lee remarried, and we were great friends of Lee and Octa in Oakland. Later, while he pastored in Frankfort, Indiana, I read an article under his name. I wrote to him and was pleased to discover he was the same Lee Nugent I had known in Oakland.

One last and most important worker: before I arrived in Oakland, Marjorie Moyer had fallen down the mission home steps and injured herself badly. Dr. and Mrs. Hill, both chiropractors, took her into their home in Oakland, where she stayed until she recovered, then she returned to the home after I had arrived there. She told us that the fall had really upset her nerves.

Haskell and Ruth Yadon had worked in the home formerly and had finished just before I arrived. Ruth and Marj were very close friends. Haskell and Ruth had taken the pastorate in Rupert, Idaho, and now visited Oakland. We formed a friendship that led to a ministerial invitation three years later.

Brother Morse had at one time belonged to the Volunteers of America, or at least one of the old Holiness groups, and had come out of that into the light of Pentecost, then on into the Name truth. Later, he had founded the work there in Oakland.

Brother Morse's ministry was unique. He had a strong burden and interest in foreign missions—that's why he had the missionary training home. The Bible college did not have today's modern prescribed curriculum. Brother Morse and other teachers held no exams, nor did they schedule certain topics at certain times. One entered the home and received whatever studies Brother Morse or others he invited gave. After breakfast on weekday mornings, students would bring their Bibles and notebooks (you didn't have to keep notes, but Marjorie had a lovely hand and we still have some beautiful notes she wrote in Ninth Street Mission in years gone by) and gather around the

91

breakfast table. Brother Morse would conduct Bible classes for a couple of hours. We'd have different lessons (Brother Morse taught on prophecy and on various subjects), and different teachers would from time to time give lessons if Brother Morris happened to be away. It all interested us and trained us, and we appreciated it.

In addition to Brother Morse, teachers included Ruby Martin, who taught on the Tabernacle, and Sister Fuller, who also helped Brother Morse quite a bit in the office. It wasn't a modern Bible college, but it did tremendously help us by teaching us and by starting us in practical experience.

I had a few dollars when I first went to the mission home but soon had to depend, like the other students, on whatever was given after the money we had at the beginning finished. Then it was a matter of going by faith, since we had no finance. Brother Morse always considered us—in fact, both he and Sister Morse were wonderful to all the young people who came into the home. Every Wednesday night offering was divided among the mission home workers. On this we depended to see us through. Of course, if someone else gave us some finances to help, we accepted and appreciated that, too. The mission people were so wonderfully good to us. Sometimes they gave food, which helped take care of our meals and shelter, but when it came to little necessities—shaving materials, haircuts, and so on—we depended on the offerings that they gave to help us over the many, many, many lean times.

Thompsee and her cat, Beauty, on the right, with friends.

Harry Morse, leader of Ninth Street Mission.

Walter Greenfeldt, who instructed Ellis in giving in Oakland, and who gave money to repair the bicycle for Joe.

Harry and Maudie Morse in the back, Elsie King and Flossie Seagraves in front.

Aunt Maud of Oakland

Marjorie Moyer

Ellis Scism ready to go to Oakland, 1930. He is 21.

CHAPTER EIGHT

Ninth Street Mission

*T*he mission gave us practical training in many ways, including having us conduct weekend meetings in the city jail. We divided into two groups. Part of this time, I led one group and Sister Chambers, the main jail ministry leader, who with her husband made a fine and very faithful couple, led the other. Neither group was allowed to minister to the women prisoners, who paid far less attention than the men. The men stayed on the twelfth floor and the women on the thirteenth. Sometimes we would minister in a portion of the jail where men stood around in an open court and other times where rows of cells stood three tiers high.

One New Year's Day the jail officials took us to a large room full of men. They opened a slot—maybe three inches by nine or ten—in the door, and a great stench came from that room. They'd just thrown these fellows in there—

whatever condition they were in when they came, that's how they lay. The number of people thrown in due to the impropriety of their New Year's celebrations left little room in the room.

Sister Mabel T. was a very unusual character. We had two Mabels in the church there: one was one of the sweetest Christians you'd ever hope to meet. Mabel T. was more volatile, more uncouth.

I did not feel it was wise for Mabel, because of some of her comments, to go to jail services, so we asked her not to go. (Her husband, Jimmy, never went anyway.) That caused quite a reaction. She had more than once said unwise things in front of the prisoners. A warning had not sufficed, and after she kept it up, I informed Sister Chambers. Mabel was very unhappy with me, but I felt this was necessary. Brother Morse and Sister Chambers both sustained my position.

We looked forward to our jail services every Sunday morning during most of my time in Oakland. We'd go down early for them, then to the mission.

One time, Alan Burgess and I ministered in the tiered section of the jail while some of the men listened. Brother Burgess felt some water on his face and couldn't figure where this came from, so he squinted and looked around and up in the top cell row. There a fellow was hiding a water pistol by his side and had been squirting it down on us as we were trying to sing to them and give them the message of life found only in the Lord Jesus Christ. Their bit of fun concluded that particular service. We held other, wonderful services in the city jail.

The jail ministry yielded results, too: some released prisoners came to Ninth Street Mission and there were baptized in water and Spirit. A few fakes showed up, too, for a handout. Sometimes it worked.

One time, a young man we had seen in jail came down to the mission, which surprised me. Come to find out, he had a scheme in his mind of going around pretending to be dumb and giving out a little printed statement to the effect that only by begging could he gain a livelihood. The police became wise to this, so they jailed him, but ultimately released him.

We also held almost daily street services. We'd carry an organ out on Ninth Street near Broadway. The wall had an electric plug, and a big light was attached to the organ frame. We'd plug the organ in, light up the corner, and stand there above the entrance to Ninth Street Mission. Quite a group of people, mostly men, would stand around. All of this, of course, differed wildly from what I'd known in my earlier years. During my time in Oakland, I gained considerable experience while doing what I could for and in behalf of the Lord's kingdom.

We also held meetings every night except Monday, and many types of services. On Wednesday night we had youth service. Night after night we'd pray with people at the altar. On some Monday nights we'd go to another church because, since we averaged getting to bed around 1:30 AM, we couldn't go to sleep anyway. Many people received the Holy Spirit.

The weekend schedule contained Saturday and Sunday afternoon and evening services. During his tenure there, Brother Morse observed the keeping of the Sabbath. Though he did not believe it was a matter of salvation, he did believe we should keep it, so he held Sabbath-keeping services at 2:00 PM on Saturday and Sabbath school on

Saturday afternoon. He also had Sunday services, also around 2:00 PM.

After returning from the city jail services, we'd go to Ninth Street Mission for our lunch, afternoon service, and evening meal. In the workers' room at the mission, we would keep our food for the day on Saturdays and Sundays, changes of clothes, hats and coats during winter, and so on. We ate our weekend afternoon and evening meals there. After a little supper, we'd have street services, then the evening service, and then prayer meetings with seekers at the altar, which lasted a long time. My first year and a half there, we averaged getting to bed about 1:30 AM, and sometimes much, much later than that. People needed prayer, and seekers wanted the Holy Spirit. We had a lot of God's work to do.

Brother Morse very conscientiously left himself very open to the Spirit's move. He would sit on the platform much of the time with his eyes closed and bounce gently up and down (his chair had springs). When someone would ask him why he sat so often with his eyes closed, he would reply that this way he could see better. Of course, he referred to sensing the Spirit's move in the meeting more than he would with eyes open.

Ninth Street Mission regularly had spiritual services, freedom in the meetings, tongues and interpretation, and all that sort of thing—wonderful meetings. Large crowds attended, with people always at the altar.

The Spirit's presence would thrill the people, who would get excited, ecstatic, and run and dance. Some who ran the aisles would open their eyes for a glance to take a turn, then go a little further and look again to take another. There was rarely a dull moment in old Ninth

Street Mission.

One night when Ardley Reynolds sat by me, the Lord moved on him and he jumped up in the air and looked as if he were going to land on me. I thought, Well, I'll see if the Lord's in it. I won't move my feet. He came down and everything was all right. Ardley later went to China, became a missionary there for many years, and did a great work for God.

One group of ladies would pray night after night in the prayer room for a real spiritual outpouring in those services. Father Nash, one of the great revivalists of that day, used to pray during the services while the evangelist was speaking. Many wonderful things took place, and God blessed many people. Many times we would see God's Spirit manifested, and when one leaves room for the Spirit of God to demonstrate, one always makes room for the unanticipated and unexpected and unhoped-for to happen.

During those years in Oakland, we saw some wonderful healings. Marjorie observed how the face of Walter Greenfeldt, after he'd had a paralyzing stroke and the people had prayed for him, straightened up after he was healed.

Walter Greenfeldt had experienced a terrible accident years before while working as an electrician and had injured his left arm, which had then been amputated above the elbow. On his right arm, he had a sense of touch only in his ring finger and little finger. He had a prosthesis, but he wouldn't use it. He'd tape his ring finger to the steering wheel when he drove.

One time he made a typical left turn without signaling. A lady driver shouted at him, "Where's your arm?" He shouted back, "At home in the trunk."

Since his one arm didn't work too well, he depended on

someone to help him button shirts and zip trousers. While he'd convalesced from the electric shock, his wife had abandoned him and married another man. Now a boy in a family of friends helped him dress himself. Since he couldn't hold a job, he received a small pension.

One day, Brother Morse had a bicycle repaired as far as his finances would permit. He asked me to go down to the mission, crate the bicycle, and send it to Brother Ardley, who needed one in China.

While I was working on it, Brother Greenfeldt came along. he wanted to know how the bicycle was. I told him, "Well, it's all right, except that the brakes are not what they should be and Brother Morse has spent all the money he can." Walter left. After a while, he came back and said, "Ellis, let's take it up to the bicycle repair shop and have the brakes repaired." He said he'd started thinking and wondered, If that were my brother in China and someone sent him a bicycle and the brakes weren't working properly and something would befall him, I would feel bad about not having done anything. So he had the brakes repaired and we sent the bicycle to China.

That experience showed me a tender spot in Walter Greenfeldt's life, heart, and mind. Some time after I left Oakland, he remarried and lived for many years. He was a great man.

Osburn Nygaard had come from Norway to the United States and worked in Oakland. A nice-looking, clean-cut, particular young man, he had a hunger for the Lord, but in his quiet way (having been a Lutheran all of his life) he found Pentecostal services too new. He'd go to the altar room to pray and first would always make sure that the crease of his trousers was just right before he knelt down.

All around him hungry and thirsty people met God in prayer. Finally, one night God gripped him and Osburn Nygaard rolled on the floor. He forgot all about the crease in his trousers and had a beautiful experience with God. Later, the war came to Europe and he went back. I have not heard anything from him for these many, many years.

Brother and Sister Carl Anderson as young folks were married at Ninth Street. Dorothy had been a missionary in China before her marriage. Many years later, she suffered a stroke or paralysis, after which she talked with difficulty and had trouble in certain hand movements. Her daughter Joy, married now, lives in Dublin, near Pleasanton, California. Her parents, last I heard, still live in Oakland. I have known them these many, many years, so a lot of memories come along that cause me to recall days passed by. Above all, God blessed and prepared me to go to India. That's why I had left home and gone to Oakland.

In those early days, when Brother and Sister Morse took their annual vacation, they invited someone to fill in for them. Once Brother and Sister Cecil Soper came, with A. D. Hurt in their car. Brother Hurt's ministry I'd experienced in Salem, and would again. The Sopers, who were musically talented, brought their marimba with vibra harp. He had been a city official in Caldwell.

While they drove along at night, Brother Hurt went to sleep and dreamed that the car had stopped, so he opened the door and got out. Of course, he had a very serious accident. The Sopers took him to a little town and the doctor helped fix him up. When he arrived in Oakland, he was still pretty banged up.

The Ninth Street Mission music was worshipful. I played the trumpet in those days (or at least tried to), so in most services I would sit near the piano and blow on the trumpet, as I continued to do even while pastoring until a front tooth's being filled ended my trumpet-playing days.

A certain brother of Italian descent whose name I never knew came to the meetings. He loved to sing and had a beautiful voice. He would start a song in the audience. I can still picture him as he would stand in old Ninth Street Mission and sing to his heart's content a song that he deeply appreciated and loved. His singing contained a strong element of worship.

Because the mission itself lay between the better, upper stratum of the town and the other, lower part, we had people who lived a better way of life—they had the income—and people down and out from the lower part of town—these were often drunks.

In those early days, I was accustomed neither to a city the size of Oakland nor to the type of people I met while there. I had many absolutely new experiences coming from Salem, Oregon, to a big city full of so many intoxicated people. I had given my heart to the Lord when just a boy and received the Holy Spirit at the age of nine, so I didn't have a clue about the outside world. I used to feel so sorry for some of the fellows down on their luck—no jobs, no place to stay.

Those were Depression years. People would approach me and ask for fifty cents, for a room, or for something like that. I gave them money for a while. I had a few dollars to start with, but that didn't take long to dwindle down. Finally Walter Greenfeldt suggested that, if I wanted to procure a room for them, not to give them the money because they would spend it on liquor or beer.

Rather, I should actually go with them to a hotel if they wanted a room or to a restaurant and pay the money there for them to get whatever they needed. I wasn't accustomed to mission work, so I took his advice and followed that principle until I ran out of finances.

Drunks often came into the meeting, and we saw the Lord's Spirit move again and again. One night, while I prayed beside a young man who would come in drunk much of the time, I noticed him shed a tear, so I told him how good it was to see him broken before the Lord, being tender towards God and all that. Then he proceeded to tell me that he didn't understand why he always had trouble with that eye. That tear duct had something wrong with it, and I hadn't noticed that he hadn't shed tears from both eyes, but just from the one. This lack of observation on my part gave me a chance to talk to him again concerning his need of God (which we had, of course, discussed previously).

In another meeting a drunk came in carrying, as always, a newspaper in his pocket. One night, I prayed and prayed with him many times. (He'd always come and want me to pray with him, and I would—again and again and again. This went on for an extended period of time.) This night I decided that I would pray and ask the Lord to save him at any cost—he'd be better off dying now and going straight to heaven without any sheaves to lay at the Master's feet than to continue in sin and die without God and without hope. So I began to pray for him that way. Finally he reached over, touched me on the arm, and told me not to pray anymore. This made me know that he wasn't too far gone to realize that he ran a risk—the Lord could answer that prayer since I certainly was concerned that he give his heart to God and not delay as he had for months.

Ninth Street was in the lower part of Oakland, yet far enough up to be not right down among the people involved in white slavery or the extreme down and out-ers—that was Sixth Street and lower.

Many mission people stood sturdily for their faith. One very pathetic story was this: some young men kidnapped two girls, Mabel Springer and another, and sold them into white slavery (forced prostitution). A madam quartered them on Sixth Street. After Mabel had lost her virginity, she was ashamed to go back to her parents. They watched and waited for her to come back, but she felt her life was ruined and they never heard from her until many years later—rather late in life.

During the meantime, Mabel married and came to the Lord. I saw her husband with her at times, but apparently by that time they had separated (I don't know why). We saw her again and again in Ninth Street Mission open-air meetings, as a member in good standing and as a beautiful Christian concerning her relationship with the Lord. She greatly benefited Ninth Street Mission work. I saw her stand out on the street service with tears streaming down her face appealing to men whom she had known when she lived in sin. Many of them with tears in their eyes would listen attentively to her plea with them to give their hearts to God. By reason of her walk with God and her love for the Lord she was known as the Angel of Broadway—a real-ly very effective and wonderful testimony.

The Depression encouraged desperate measures by peo-ple needing jobs. Harold Bergman told me that, when he had such a hard time getting a job, a sideshow came through his town and offered him a job as the Wild Woman of Borneo. They put him in a cage, yet not as thoroughly protected as he might have been, and in a wig of disheveled hair. They kept little chickens around, and he was supposed to be sucking the blood out of them. An American Indian man came, watched, and finally reached through the partition and grabbed Brother Bergman's hair to find out, of course, that the Wild Woman of Borneo was a white Anglo-Saxon Protestant male. Then the show fixed up the cage so that no one could reach in and grab the hair of whoever might be advertised as the Wild Woman of Borneo. Later he joined the Assemblies of God.

Ninth Street Mission didn't get that strange, but had its characters. One elderly man used to wear a robe with many verses of Scripture written on it. I understood that he had been at one time a member of the Seventh-day Adventist Church and had been in so much trouble that he had been dropped by them. He would stand on the street in his robe, carry an American flag, and talk against Mussolini, whom he called Macaroni. I used to stand once in a while and listen to part of his harangue because he did it right there in front of old Ninth Street Mission when we were not having open-air services.

One old black man, Silas, had a horizontal board fixed to the front bumper of the Model T Ford sedan someone had given him. He'd use this as a platform for street sermons—to preach and play the guitar. Once when he'd attracted a crowd, he laid his Bible on the Model T hood. One fellow snitched the Bible, hid it under his coat, and walked off. He then stood in a spot down the street just to see what Silas would do. Silas went to his toolbox, got a tire iron, and recovered his Bible.

Silas would come to Ninth Street Mission now and then. One time he came in looking for a chair and knelt down in front of Brother Morse's. Brother Morse's platform was usually filled with helpers in the Ninth Street work, and he would always sit in a certain chair. When Brother Morse came from the office a little later than normal and found his place already occupied, he handled it very deftly and naturally provided another chair, which he invited Brother Silas to sit in, and Brother Silas did.

Brother Childs's brother-in-law, Brother Andros, came from San Francisco for an afternoon meeting, probably Sunday. He gave quite a lengthy Bible lecture. Brother Silas started out by saying, "Bless him, Lord. Bless him, Lord. Help him, Lord. Help 'im." As the speaker went on, seeming to receive considerable help and kept on and on preaching, finally the old brother said, "Have mercy, have mercy, Lord. Have mercy." Ultimately, he could not take it too much longer because the speaker seemed to get along so well and carry on such a lengthy discourse that finally Silas rose, walked off the platform, down one of the aisles, and out the door. Apparently he thought the Lord had answered his first prayer more than anticipated. Silas, for the last half hour he had been sitting, had been ill.

This same Silas would, while he was speaking, remove his dentures, wipe them with his used handkerchief, and reinsert them in his mouth. This procedure fascinated me.

One evening after a large crowd had gathered at Ninth Street Mission, three or four boys of foreign descent from the pugilistic school in Hayward came and began to comment improperly about some of the girls just as the meeting was to start. Someone informed the deputy, so he went over to them and asked them not to make such comments, plainly indicating that they were welcome but that they must respect Ninth Street Mission as a place of worship.

They became very obstinate and unkind toward him. Finally he showed them his badge indicating that the city had deputized him. They said they could buy those for ten cents or twenty-five cents at the pawn shop. He prepared to show them out after they said that, when they began to give him short jabs. They hit him in the nose. When his heart would beat, his nose would spurt blood. That, of course, put him out of the race. By this time the meeting had started.

Then Miles Ringle, Walter Hogan, and Joe Borocco came over and took those boys under control. All these men had experience in boxing and really cleared the place out. Miles Ringle had been a fighter and was now a faithful church member with his parents and his wife, Ruth. Joe Borocco, I believe, said to these lads, "Don't you stick up your mitts to me." He'd been saved out of the city jail. Walter Hogan hit one of the boys, and it didn't take long to end, although there was an aftermath since the police had to be notified. We had some unfortunate experiences.

One night they asked me to serve as substitute bouncer. The city never had deputized me like they had the officially appointed bouncers for the mission—old Daddy Hills and Harry Hopkins occupied that job for a long time. This night at young people's meeting, one black fellow came in and stood around one of the two entrances into the mission. He started taking off some of his apparel, so I went back and asked him to stop and to put his clothing back on. He put his hand in his hip pocket. What he had actually gone for was his pipe, but I had no way of knowing that he might not be reaching for something a bit sharper.

One man came to me after service and said, "Blacks are known for carrying razors around. If a black man causes problems, don't hit him in the head. Kick him in the shins." That was his way of looking at it.

Some of those old Ninth Street experiences might not be what we preferred in a place of worship, but they happened, and in the midst of it all God blessed. Many were baptized in Jesus' name, were filled with the Holy Spirit, and met God in a wonderful way.

Once Sister Cassie tried to illustrate the concept of unity. Old Ninth Street Mission had experienced a little friction and crowds had fallen off somewhat. Brother Morse always invited a number of workers to his platform, though they always respected his chair, with the exception of one time, as already mentioned.

This night, Sister Cassie, under the presumed touch of the Lord's Spirit, began pulling two heads together, and kept doing this coming down the line. I began to figure out the situation. It so happened that on my right a certain young lady was sitting. I figured out that if Sister Cassie didn't stop doing this before she came as far as our seats, she'd pull my head toward this girl's and hers toward mine. But the Lord was in it all, and Sister Cassie stopped before she reached us.

One time I was asked to lead a meeting when Matt R. Tatman was to speak. Sometimes he preached for us and sometimes for The Apostolic Faith (a three-works-of-grace group headquartered at a big church on Duke Street in Portland, Oregon) or for whomever else might invite him. Years before, I'd heard him preach in Salem for a couple of weeks, and at least thirty-three people had received the Holy Spirit in a trinitarian church. We called him "the Cyclone Preacher." People throughout North America knew him by this title. Very demonstrative and quite bald, a former sleight-of-hand performer, and a rather acrobatic individual, he would perspire freely, speak with fervor, wipe his handkerchief on his bald head, and then throw it in the audience.

He and his wife, Maggie, had helped Brother Morse, but then, for a period of years, they'd had troubles between them and the Morses, so they'd left and now were struggling financially. Brother Morse felt sorry for them and took up an offering to help them in their need. Brother Morse always took the lead in trying to correct any situation that might arise, and always seemed to hope that things would improve next time. The same thing happened more than once. They requested forgiveness from Brother and Sister Morse, and Brother Morse again invited him down to preach.

This night, a certain man and woman came in. They had been drinking and caused quite a commotion. The people asked me to talk to them, so I did, particularly to the lady, but also to the man. She said, "I don't want him to make a disturbance." Of course, I explained that they were welcome to the mission but that they must not cause a disturbance in the meeting.

This was during the sermon. As Brother Tatman kept speaking and really having a great time going through quite a few acrobatics, finally the performance overcame our visitor, who jumped to his feet and shouted out, "Boy, how you could sell beer!" That was the beginning of the end, causing quite a crowd reaction, because people could see the funny side. They knew the man was intoxicated, and the final outcome for such people was that they had to leave, which they did. We helped them vacate the premises—out the door and up the steps. Things like this took place many times in old Ninth Street Mission.

One time, a man came down into the mission with three or four dogs on leashes. Of course, he too had to leave.

Another one of the characters, some fellow who claimed to be Elijah come back or Isaiah, tried to take over the meeting one night. Finally, Brother Morse just told him to sit down. The power of God hit him and he hit the floor. Brother Morse had once again kept himself open toward the moving of the Spirit in the services, and he conducted his ministry this way down through the years— it didn't simply come along as something new. Because he allowed great freedom in the Spirit, he had great authority in the Spirit, and we saw God's Spirit move.

Mabel Springer, the Angel of Broadway.

CHAPTER NINE

Romance, Courtship, Marriage

*O*nce, Thompsee, the retired lady who had transferred her house title to Brother Morse, traveled with me up to Oregon—she on vacation, me to visit my folks. I dropped her off at Oregon City, then drove on to my folks' place in Salem. She visited Marjorie Moyer's family and another family in Oregon City. She thought a lot of Marjorie.

Marjorie planned to return to Oakland, so Thompsee wanted to know if we all three could ride back together in the Model T Ford coupe. Of course, that worked out very well. We drove down the Redwoods Road, while Marj and I had a chance to get better acquainted and enjoy each other's company. Of course, I could tell that Thompsee had pretty well formulated in her mind that I should marry Marjorie and, of course, that worked out. I appreciated Thompsee's concern and effort.

As time went by, Marjorie and I saw each other at the mission home now and then. The house rules said that a young man and young lady should not pair off or go out by themselves, but should go out in a group. We obeyed these prohibitions, but we did have a strong attraction to each other.

Sister Morse once told me that, had she not known the house rules, she would have wondered whether we thought as much of each other as we should in order to get married. She recognized that we were trying to obey the rules of the home, which we were, and in which effort we succeeded.

One time, Walter Greenfeldt took Marj and me down to the beach. While we talked and visited with Walter, Marj and I held hands under the sand. I don't know whether he knew what was going on or not. At any rate, there are ways in which one can indicate concern one for the other.

After church one night, we came to the mission home, and while upstairs in the kitchen having a bite—just the two of us—like good Northwesterners we expressed our concern for each other (that expression involves quite a bit). We were now engaged and decided to inform Brother and Sister Morse.

I was very, very poor; I had no money to buy clothes or a wedding ring. This was 1932. I decided that, since I had no funds to buy new clothes, I would get married in the suit and shoes I wore for services. That was an easy decision. Concerning the wedding ring, I didn't know what to do.

The church people, as always, treated us very kindly. Sister Louise Olsen arranged a shower for Marjorie, and many ladies gathered at Sister Olsen's place. They invited me to go over as well, which I did. Come to find out, they had arranged to take up a special offering for me at that shower, apparently with the thought that the money would help me buy a ring for Marjorie.

Buying a ring during the Depression differed somewhat from today's practice, and I could scarcely take on such a monumental task. Naturally, the offering didn't have enough money to buy a nice ring. Marjorie and I went down to an Oakland pawn shop where I bought a silver ring pawned by someone. That became Marjorie's wedding ring until after we went to India. There, we visited Kottayam to see some jewelers, and I ordered a twenty-two _tola_ (heavier than a karat) gold wedding ring for Marjorie, which helped to make up for the years when she did not have a wedding ring like I wanted her to have. I had her name engraved on the inside of the wedding band. Though it was not marked with gems, it did signify that we cared for and loved each other. That ring she still wore when she passed away.

The night came for the wedding—19 September 1932. My mother and dad could not attend, but Marjorie's sister, Ferne, could. She worked in Oakland and later became Ferne Greene. Marj and I named our daughter after her. Ferne Moyer was the maid of honor. Osburn Nygaard, who had received the Holy Ghost in Ninth Street Mission, was the best man. Marjorie's brother Ordell attended, as did Dr. McCullough and his wife. She sang at the wedding.

Brother Morse united us in marriage. Louise Olsen and her friends of the Forget-Me-Not Missionary Circle arranged a room in a hotel for Marjorie and me to spend our first night. After the wedding ceremony and our part in the reception ended, the Olsens came and told us it was time to go. We slipped away. People realized, of course, that we were going, but no one was supposed to know where. The Olsens took us to a hotel in Oakland.

After we got to our room, someone let the information out as to where we were, so quite a group of people came to the hotel and wanted to get in touch with us. They pestered the man at the desk and inquired as to whether Mr. and Mrs. Scism were present.

The telephone rang. When Marjorie answered and they wanted to know who she was, she forgot that she'd been married, and said her name was Marjorie Moyer. Then the people knew they had the right line.

During the meantime, a friend of ours downstairs recognized Ordell's truck. He was in the room serving us ice cream and cake. Our downstairs friend stood by the truck and made a sound like air escaping from the tire. When Ordell heard this noise he stuck his head out the window. Then they knew which room was ours. Ultimately, we permitted them to come up, providing they did not stay very long. Quite a group trooped up to our room and tried to play a trick on us while they were there—shortening the sheets or something. We had to pull the bed down off the wall after moving chairs out of the way to make space.

Eventually, the Olsens and everyone else left. Then Marj and I settled down to our first night.

Martha Solkell, a congenial soul who owned one of the cabins by Clear Lake, had invited Marj and me to go there for our honeymoon. Brother and Sister Morse owned another of those cabins, which they used to visit on vacation times (Sister Morse would go up between vacation times as well). Marj and I invited the Reznicseks and Sister

Morse to go up with us on our honeymoon. People teased me, of course, about having outside people go with us on our honeymoon, but I thought it was a good idea; Marjorie wanted it, too. It worked out well and we all had a good time together.

The day after the wedding, we loaded up the Model T Ford coupe and started for Clear Lake Oaks. The Reznicseks and Sister Morse went in Joe's Dodge. Although I'd really loaded the Model T well in back, it made good time on the level and downhill would really move along. However, on the uphill climb, it would slow down and the Reznicseks would catch up and pass us. Sometimes we'd look back and see no sign of them anywhere. On one occasion, we climbed a hill and look back at the level area to see them way down there. Of course, soon they passed us. Most of the time, that little Model T could make good speed, and we enjoyed it, especially on our honeymoon.

One day, before Brother Morse arrived, the whole crowd of us rowed in a boat to an island on the other side of the lake, climbed a hill, and ate a lot of figs. In the afternoon, we drove in Brother Reznicsek's car to a mineral water spring. Brother Reznicsek and I decided to see who could drink the most mineral water. We worked on the project, but I just could not drink as much of it as he could. Its flavor did not suit me at all. On the way back, he took sick and vomited. We had a lot of fun teasing him, knowing that the mixture of figs and mineral water did not set in a very favorable situation in his stomach.

We appreciated the presence of Brother and Sister Reznicsek, with whom we have enjoyed many good times. While we were there, Brother Morse came up later and we took pictures. It was a wonderful vacation—very restful and encouraging, a very lovely time and so pleasant to be together for those few days. All too soon, the time came to return to Oakland and to our duties and responsibilities there.

We entered quickly back into the work. During the intervening years from our wedding until we left Oakland in August 1934, when Harry was just a little baby, we assumed more responsibility in the mission and home since we were more senior workers than when we first came.

Marj went not only to city jail services but also to the county jail with some of the older sisters at Ninth Street. She enjoyed ministering in those services. On a couple of occasions after we were married, I took her to the county jail.

Peter D. came to Oakland after Marjorie and I were married. Before she had come to Oakland, Peter had visited her home church and talked to Brother Andrew Baker against the Bible school. He had mentioned that the school was located in the part of town where at times disreputable characters would invite the young girls out. He had expressed concern that this might happen to Marj, so Brother Baker had talked to Marjorie about it and told her what Peter had said.

After Marjorie had gone down to Oakland before I ever went there, Peter had come down and, lo and behold!, was the first one to ask her out. Later, after Marjorie and I married, again Peter came that way, this time very perturbed and shaking his head that night. I can't recall all the circumstances just now, but I do remember him expressing displeasure as Marjorie and I walked across the street together.

When Joseph Reznicsek came back from India on a furlough, he was speaking in a meeting in the Northwest when he saw a person sitting in the congregation sticking his head out from behind someone. This person would keep looking toward the platform, then move back out of sight again. Finally, the fact that this was Peter dawned on Brother Reznicsek, so he made it a point to contact Peter after the service.

Peter had stayed in the home of a pastor whom Joe had also visited. The pastor told Joe that Peter had visited during a cold time of year when the pastor did not have enough bedding or quilts to put on the bed, so he suggested that Peter put the pastor's overcoat on the bed to help keep him warmer during the night. The next day, after Peter had left, the pastor found out that he had taken the overcoat and also some underwear. Apparently Peter thought of this as he looked toward the platform and recognized Joseph Reznicsek.

Peter had quite a checkered history along the way. He had been married at one time, but things had not worked out too well for him.

Once Bert B., a happy-go-lucky individual, preached up a storm at the mission. The workers called him "Bert Whiz-bang." He gave his invitation and told the people that, no matter what was wrong with them, to come up and he would pray them through. No one went.

Of course, he felt that everything was okay regarding himself, but the next day he ran into a little disagreement. Every time he parked his car, he'd bump a hedge belonging to Brother Morse's neighbor. Brother Morse called him into the office to talk with him, and this brother lost what equilibrium he possessed. Later he told me himself that he

117

was tempted to punch Brother Morse—he didn't hit him, of course, but he lost his victory. That night on the way down to the mission in the worker's car, Bert said, "Last night I could pray them through and tonight I need them to pray me through." A lot of things went on in old Ninth Street Mission long, long ago.

Jimmy and Mabel T. used to make life interesting for everyone around them. They'd come back into the church, then leave, then come back, then leave, and had now returned again. Jimmy could preach well, looked nice, had a pleasant personality, and had prayed successfully for people's healing, but we found out years later that all along Jimmy and Mabel had had their problems. He would go away somewhere all day, then come back just before a meeting that night. They'd quarrel, then iron out things, go to the meeting, and have a good time.

These and other incidents influenced my life to make me know that not everyone we see in church is pleasing to God. Under the surface a completely different situation can prevail. How much better it is to live for the Lord twenty-four hours a day than just to be off and on, as does happen occasionally, though thankfully, not too often.

At old Ninth Street Mission, Brother Morse left me in charge of the service one night. I had asked someone to speak, and Jimmy was very displeased with whomever was speaking. He came to me and said he could preach them down, and as far as preaching goes, unquestionably he could. The questionable part, and his ministry's number one problem, was whether he could live what he preached.

So Mabel one night in the prayer room prayed loud enough for me to hear what she said: "Lord, help those who think they are better than others."

One day during these last years in Oakland, while walking between services on one street, I heard someone shouting, "N.R.A.! N.R.A.! If you don't like Roosevelt, you better keep your mouth shut." The little old man who always preached against Mussolini, calling him Macaroni, apparently was not on too good terms with the president. Apparently this man considered the National Recovery Act to be an administrative forerunner of the mark of the beast. Franklin Delano Roosevelt's programs did a good job during those days, though he also came in for his portion of criticism.

Sister Cassie, mentioned earlier, also labored under a great burden regarding the N.R.A. being the mark of the beast. I remember one night that she, under a great deal of stress, walked back and forth in front of the platform, giving a direct prophecy in English, warning the people not to have anything to do with the National Recovery Act because it was the mark of the beast. That, of course, did not prove to be factual, but at least it portrays again the unusual things that happened in old Ninth Street Mission. I found Sister Cassie to be so honest and a wonderful person, though she may have missed it now and then.

We must bear in mind, where the Spirit of the Lord is allowed freedom, sometimes this is taken advantage of. I heard Sister Cassie say one time that, when you are anointed in giving an interpretation of a message, it's so easy to go on beyond the actual interpretation of the message and speak out on your own. And I've observed this to be entirely too true. It happens at times. Still, it's better to be pliable and useful in God's hands than to be contrary and miss every opportunity to do what one can to witness in the Spirit for the Lord.

During the summer of 1933, when Marjorie was early in her first pregnancy, Brother Morse and I set the grass and leaves of the vacant lot next door to the home on fire to burn them off to prevent accidental fire later. While we were there, we sat down to rest because it was hot work. The smoke from the burning leaves billowed over onto the clothesline at the home, which meant that Marjorie would have to do the washing all over again to get the smoke out of the sheets. Sister Morse came to the rescue of Marjorie and remonstrated with Brother Morse for having burned leaves when washing was on the line. After she left, Brother Morse observed that even as Maudie Morse had more brindle than he did, Marjorie had more brindle than I did—I was more laid back—and he wondered whether the coming baby would have more brindle or less. As it turned out, he had more.

On August 25, 1933, Marjorie and I were ordained to the ministry at the Western District conference of the Pentecostal Ministerial Alliance. Brother Morse was then an official in that organization.

While we were in Oakland, Sister Tiny, who seemed to have much influence as a prophetess, once came to Marjorie and me after we were married and concluded that the Lord had showed her great things for us. According to her, God wanted us to go east to Chicago, where God would give us a wonderful ministry and a great harvest of souls. Of course, we never did go to Chicago. God had called us to India, where we went after a time. That's why we prepared in Oakland. We never even visited Chicago until years later while home on furlough when we visited Brother Hildebrand. We have gone there a few times since, to his church and others in the Chicago area, but only during our time of missionary service in India.

Not all who say they have the mind of Christ or the leading of the Holy Spirit actually do, yet that does not annul the fact that God does lead individuals to help others know or feel God's leading. Each individual must be strong in the Word, feel in his own heart what God would have him do, then be willing to follow the Holy Spirit's leading to further the work of God's kingdoms in his life.

Some time between our marriage and the trip with Joe and Faith, Marj and I took care of Joseph Arthur, Joe's boy by Gladys. As mentioned earlier, Mother McCarty had returned him to my neighborhood in Howell, Oregon. Of course, by this time the erstwhile little fellow had grown somewhat older. Soon we would scamper across the country with his dad and stepmother.

Harry Morse, Ellis Scism, and Joe Rezniscek at Ellis Scism's honeymoon.

121

CHAPTER TEN

The Journey with Joe and Faith

*L*ater in 1933, Marjorie and I took an extended missionary journey with Joe and Faith Reznicsek. Marj and I planned to go to India but we did not know when. Yet, since that was our objective, we traveled with these Indian missionaries in Joe's Dodge on a nine-thousand-plus-mile trip. We tied the suitcases on the running board of the Dodge with a canvas around them.

We left California's fair weather, and on Oregon's wet pavement the rear end skidded into a curb. In those days, wheels had wooden spokes. We had knocked a wheel out of alignment, which caused it to wobble, so we installed some Babbitt, a solid substance put in the wheel hub to align a single wheel.

After repairs, we journeyed on to Idaho. In our group, my wife and Faith played their guitars, Joe a saxophone, and I the trumpet. Of course, Joe was the main speaker.

Marj and I were fledglings getting our experience. At the same time, Marj was pregnant with Harry. (He was born the following March after we had completed the trip.) That journey with Joe and Faith gave us some wonderful experiences—as far as the car was concerned, some favorably interesting times and some not so nice.

By the time we reached Idaho and had stopped here and there with several flat tires between Boise and Twin Falls (one of the beads had broken—I don't know how many flats we had on that thing), we finally came near Glens Ferry, Idaho. We had put the broken-beaded tire back on, but it blew in no time. As a result, we parked by the roadside.

Brother Reznicsek told me he would go on and see if a tire was available. I was to follow him at a distance and carry the rim. If I saw him leave any particular place, I would still follow at a distance. We walked clear through the little town of Glens Ferry until he came to a wrecking yard. Then he didn't come out, so I went in. He had found an old tire with a small hole, but they had sold him a boot to put inside the tire and that was the only thing available in the whole place. We bought it and continued our journey into Twin Falls late where we were supposed to spend the night with Brother and Sister Haskell Yadon.

After a few days with them, we then spent a few days in Rupert. During our two-day visit there, we drove up to Albion and went jack rabbit hunting. I was so weary that when I sat on the platform that night, I unfortunately dozed off. Just then in my dream a great, big jackrabbit jumped across right in front of me. I told Dale Walker's father about it (Dale was then a small boy), and he loved to tease me about it later. We continued traveling to our next scheduled stop—Northphlet, Arkansas, with Brother and Sister Pair. Unfortunately, we did not arrive on schedule because of the tire trouble. In Northphlet, Brother Pair took two tires off his car and put them on Brother Reznicsek's car. That certainly took care of our tire problem.

During this time we attended the conference of the Pentecostal Ministerial Alliance (PMA) held in Louisiana, Missouri. Brother A. D. Hurt chaired that particular conference. (They rotated the chairmanship in those days.)

Brother W. E. Kidson, secretary of the PMA, had arranged to house the conference at an old hotel he owned in Louisiana, Missouri. Nowadays someone might have accused Brother Kidson of scheduling the conference where he owned a hotel so that he could profit personally from the conference, but ministers' mentality was different back then.

Of course, Joe and I had no money and were trying to work our way along by doing what we could to help. At the hotel, I had quite an undertaking: I was asked to take care of the hotel furnace, while Brother Reznicsek oversaw the furnace where the meetings were being conducted. I had no end of trouble trying to take care of the furnace. It was coal fired, and I was used to wood. Coal burns hotter, and you have to bank it (shovel dirt up in front to break the draft) to hold the heat through the night. The dirt was readily available—the building had a cellar, not a basement.

One night, I came in to find water all over one part of the dirt floor near the furnace. Who was responsible? I was not the only one taking care of this furnace. Since the water pressure was quite high, the oil boiler had burst.

Other problems also arose. For example, the sinks

plugged up in one or more of the rooms (I don't remember exactly how many now). I went down in the basement in my blue sweater and unscrewed one pipe plug in order to insert a wire. Suddenly, that rusty water rushed down, got me soaking wet, and ruined my sweater. I couldn't buy sweaters easily.

They had to remove the wall to install another used furnace. Brother Kidson announced that the old furnace was ruined and that he did not want anything like this to happen again. At any rate, this added to our experience. Then we went on down to the state of Louisiana, and then to Houston.

At one of the Houston churches, the pastor's wife led the song service that night, standing by the piano while we played our instruments. When this sister led, they really sang full speed ahead.

We continued from Houston around different parts of Texas until we started back home. Just east of Albuquerque we ran into a norther. The wind, ice, and snow, coupled with the muddy roads, left us in a bad, freezing situation in the middle of nowhere. We arrived at remote gas stations in the wee hours of the morning when they'd been long closed and finally, very low on gas, stopped at a station up on the pass in the early morning hours. A lady came out in nightgown, nightcap, and coat and declared up and down that she didn't have any gasoline. We could do nothing but drive on and hope for the best.

In these few minutes, the slush and ice collected around the tie rod had frozen. We got out, knocked it off, and coasted down until we landed in the yard of Brother and Sister Dale Struble's home.

Those were rough Depression days, so when our time

126

came to leave, the offering was small and we had a long way to go—to Rupert, Idaho. Brother Struble had managed to provide some gasoline in a tin. We carried that along with us to refill the tank.

We stopped in Denver hoping that we would be able to borrow some money from Sister Reznicsek's brother. We could borrow hardly anything—two dollars. We continued toward Idaho. Naturally, our eating was limited. All we had was salami and bread.

On our way through the mountains in Wyoming, one of the connecting rods gave way, and all we could do was put the canvas down to make a windbreak from the cold wind blowing across the plains. We weighted the canvas down with rocks and crawled under to remove the pan. Brother Reznicsek took sick and then asked me to crawl under, which I did. We fortunately had another portion of a connecting rod, so we put it on, which did not completely cure the situation by any means, but it did make the engine run until we could get into a town.

By this time we were completely out of money, so Brother Reznicsek pawned his watch to a man who ran a service station in the next town and assured the man that he would send the money for it after arriving in Rupert. The man gave us some gasoline and some used oil, which we put in the motor. Then we had ten dollars to go to a restaurant and buy liver and onions. That was our first hot meal in a long, long time, and it sure tasted good. After our meal that evening, we continued our journey to Rupert, arriving late again, but much closer to the end of our extended missionary journey.

Brother Reznicsek sent the money for the watch, but never did receive it back again, so it was a total loss. Of course, the value of the watch far exceeded the amount that he had received for it that day—$10 plus gasoline and old oil. The service station man apparently recognized he had a good thing when he saw it.

On this journey we had the joy of visiting Bill Maulden in his home mission church. It was a beautiful service, but he was not there very long. I would work with him when I pastored in Tieton, then later on church business in Caldwell in 1944 and in the merger in 1945, then in the work in Superior and in Billings, Montana, then in Portland. The Mauldens also lived in Caldwell for a while before moving back to Yakima. When we meet new people, we don't know what great new friendships these casual introductions will bring.

We continued on and ultimately returned to Oakland. Soon afterward, the Reznicseks left for India, while Marj and I reentered the work in Harry Morse's Ninth Street Mission.

Rev. and Mrs. Allen Burgess on the left, Joe and Faith Rezniscek on the right.

CHAPTER ELEVEN

Our Last Nine Months in Oakland

*S*ome time after Marj and I returned from the journey with Joe and Faith, Brother Morse unwisely counseled a young woman alone in his office. Two very influential preachers brought against him accusations of immorality far out of proportion to his indiscretion, even alerting the newspapers and Earl Warren, prosecuting attorney in Oakland. Brother Morse, gentle as always, said of the two men, "They're my friends." They weren't his friends at all.

For a while as the gossip raged, the attendance decidedly slumped, the people went through a time of great discouragement, and so the Spirit's demonstration diminished. This extreme problem made everything very difficult for a time.

During that particular onslaught of the adversary over the work's progress, one time while we workers all prayed in the prayer room with Brother Morse, a woman started causing a disturbance outside. She said she was an evangelist and wanted to hold a revival for Brother Morse. She had been with the Foursquare people in the southern part of the state and had come up to Oakland. They called her Hitchhiking Mary.

Brother Morse took one look at her and knew she was not an individual he would welcome as an evangelist in the mission, so he gave her no encouragement whatsoever and, in fact, refused. Even so, she would still come down to Ninth Street, and during those difficult days when the crowds were generally poor, the mission struggled, and the workers and a few saints and Brother Morse prayed in the prayer room, she would stand around outside talking with some of the hangers-on, berating Brother Morse and making a lot of noise with the men out there.

Finally, after listening to this in the midst of his praying, Brother Morse couldn't absorb any more, so he got up and left the prayer room. When he came back in, we wondered what had happened. He commented that he'd cast out a demon. He'd escorted her out from the mission, made Mary hitchhike out of the church basement.

In the end, that particular situation worked out, as people saw that the accusations were false. I remained loyal to Brother Morse through it all, and still am, as many people were and are.

On March 8, 1934, the day before Harry was born, Marjorie stayed in the bedroom in the home. I deposited myself in another room because Marjorie was due. Early the next morning, Harry was born. Doctor Dobyns put string and bacon down Harry's throat to cut the phlegm, gave him a couple of slaps, and he (Harry, not the doctor) emitted a cry.

After I left the room, a young man sharing it came back from church. He did not want to wake me by turning the light on, so he felt his way in the dark. When he could not find me, he concluded that the Lord had come and taken me and left him.

On March 21, 1934, Harry was twelve days old and about to be dedicated. I was going to bring him from the home in my Model T Ford coupe, but Brother Morse wanted me to take his Willys Knight. I borrowed it, drove out to the home, and was bringing Harry back to the night service when, lo and behold, a motorcycle policeman stopped me. I had forgotten my speed because the motor of Brother Morse's car was very quiet. With a Model T, I would listen to the noise and guess how fast we were going, but I couldn't do that with a Willys Knight. The result was I didn't watch the speed on her like I should have, got a ticket, and later on had to appear in court.

I took Harry down to the mission, where Brother Harry Morse dedicated him to the Lord. Our son was named after him.

Regarding the traffic ticket, Brother Morse came to my rescue, called me into the office, gave me a talking-to, and signed a blank check. That's how I received what turned out to be the five dollars to pay the fine for speeding.

One night not too long after the dedication, in walked one of the drunks who occasionally came. I'd seen him around a number of times at street meetings and all, and I mentioned to him that we had a baby. He was so delighted and said, "When I see him, I'm going to lay a five-dollar bill on him."

I told the drunk, "Stay right here and I'll bring Harry out." We used to take Harry down in a basket. He'd sleep

131

in it while Marjorie and I sat on the platform, until he needed attention. At the moment, he was sleeping in the workers' room. The drunk hadn't anticipated that Harry would be there that night and, of course, he never did lay the five dollars on him, but the opportunity to let him know Harry's availability was too good to pass up.

Then came Brother Glenn Cook, one of the old-timers in Pentecost from the early days of the outpouring. He had held the first Jesus Name baptismal service east of the Mississippi River, baptizing Brother L. V. Roberts. Brother Homer White gave me a picture of that first baptismal service when we visited him on deputation in 1955-56, years before his death.

Brother and Sister Morse had gone up to Clear Lake for their vacation, I had been left in charge, and I could sense that something—I didn't know just what God had in mind for that particular service—was in the offing. Brother Cook, sitting beside me, said he thought the people hesitated to testify because they wanted to hear him preach. I didn't feel that way about it, though I didn't know.

Finally, after some delay, I went ahead and introduced him briefly to the congregation (he had visited before). Then someone broke out into tongues, and it was not the Spirit, but a rebuke. Brother Morse had taught the people that, as the pastor, he would do any rebuking that should or would be done. One of the young men really missed it that night. Finally, I had to take a strong hand to correct the situation, and told the young man to sit down. At any rate, Brother Cook was not able to go ahead until a little later on in the service.

A few months later, the Teamsters went on strike. One time they tipped a gasoline truck over, and gasoline ran down through the gutter along the street. Many of the strikers came to Ninth Street. Again, Brother and Sister Morse were away at the time, leaving Marj and me in charge of the work during their absence.

One of the men who worked at a shoe store in town told me that milk might be scarce because the Teamsters had stopped supplying milk to stores and hospitals. He said that if I would buy groceries, he would pay for them. We went through the line and bought quite a number of tins of Carnation milk. When we left Oakland in August, not long after, we put that milk on the car's running board as we traveled north.

I'd had the Model T when Marjorie and I were married in Oakland and all the time since, but now it was going the way of all flesh. Allan Burgess was working for the Atlas Glass and Furnace Company when a gas furnace blew up. We went to see him several times. At first he didn't think he'd live—he was so badly crippled—but after he did pull through, he received many forms to help him with the company's disability insurance. He gave us two hundred dollars, with which we bought a 1927 Dodge sedan. That happened not too long before we left Oakland. This 1927 Dodge I drove to Salem.

Now, sixty years later, Oakland has undergone such drastic change that it is difficult to recognize as the same place. Time marches on, life moves ahead, and the souls of people are that much nearer to the coming of Christ.

I appreciate my years in Oakland very, very much. Especially to someone like me coming from a small town, the knowledge and expertise gained there and the blessings gained in the services benefited work later. I appreciate Brother Morse's ministry, his Bible teaching, his leadership both at the home and in the mission, and the many nights of prayer. I have no regrets about having gone. He was a great man who in his later days unfortunately went in with a group that led him away from truths that our brethren have stood for these many years. Nonetheless, his life greatly benefited our lives. We experienced much in old Ninth Street Mission, occasions which we now remember and by which we have been greatly blessed.

CHAPTER TWELVE

Clarkston

By August 1934, Marjorie and I felt that time had come for us to make our move, so with our little baby boy we packed up and loaded down our 1927 four-door Dodge sedan, tied our tins of Carnation milk to the bumper, and left Oakland, heading north into a future we neither knew nor understood. We went, some would say, blind.

We didn't think too much about what might happen to that milk. Unfortunately, it soured due to the heat, so we lost it.

As we headed north, we stopped for a bite to eat in a little place among the redwoods. We were hungry, yet there was this matter of finances and we had a long distance to travel, so Marjorie ordered soup and also started eating lots of the pretzels they kept available there. Finally, the waiter came around and removed the pretzel jar.

I don't remember too much about that trip, except that we didn't make too much speed. The journey took a few days, the same amount of time as it had taken me when I first went down to Oakland. The trip was much better than when I drove the Model T Ford because that time we'd gone a more direct route, whereas this time we took the very crooked Redwood Highway (101). We went that way because we'd seen part of the redwood forest coming back from Oregon City with Thompsee and wanted to see the beautiful trees again.

We wended our way up to Salem and stopped to visit my parents for a while. At that time, my brother and his wife, Maybelle, still lived there.

Dad was not one to exclaim very much over becoming a grandparent, but Mother was more expressive.

At a mealtime during this visit, Dad once said at the table, "Toss me a biscuit" (Mom made good, old-fashioned biscuits that we all loved), so I picked up one and tossed it to him. This surprised him, not to speak of Marjorie. Then he took off after me. I knew he was coming my direction, so I left the table and ran at top speed outside. Dad threw a rawhide chair at me. It didn't make contact with me, just banged against the door. This introduced Marjorie to her in-laws.

Later on, we visited Marjorie's mother and family in Oregon City. They didn't throw chairs or even rolls.

During the meantime, we had decided to attend the Northwestern District conference in Caldwell, Idaho, where Brother and Sister Rohn pastored. At this writing about sixty years later, Brother Rohn still pastors there. We started out around midnight; we wanted to save motel expense. Mother Moyer exhorted Marjorie to make sure I stayed awake. She assured her mother that she would, and she did.

By the time we reached the Bonneville area, I was so drowsy that I pulled over to the side of the road to get some rest. Suddenly the construction workers at the Bonneville Dam dumped a huge load of rock and woke me up, so I couldn't sleep. The natural conclusion was to keep on driving, so I started up the Dodge and we went on.

Marjorie had Harry on her lap and she became drowsy, too. It was difficult for both of us—one time Marjorie almost let Harry slip off her lap. Finally we arrived in Caldwell and found a place to stay with friends there.

At the conference, Haskell and Ruth Yadon asked us to go to Rupert with them afterward and they would see what they could do to help me locate a place. We agreed, and traveled from Caldwell to Rupert with them.

We've been warm friends of theirs these many, many years since. When Marjorie died in 1983, I asked Haskell Yadon to speak at the funeral. This he did, coming all the way to Portland from his home in Caldwell. Ruth died in 1993.

We had visited with Joe and Faith for a few days the year before, but now we spent several months with them in Rupert, helping them and doing what we could to assist in the church. We would sweep the church building, scrub it from time to time, and start fires. We'd go out in the desert and procure sagebrush—heating the house in winter was costly, so we depended a lot on sagebrush being brought in from time to time in Haskell's trailer. During the harvest season, we would dig up carrots with Brother Clayton, Winton Walker, and some others.

The dust bowl apparently reached clear to Idaho. One

time, Haskell and I and Percy MacKenzie, who drove, went out into the desert for a service for people living in an outpost. Prior to our leaving, Sister Walker suggested we take drinking water along in a half-gallon jar. We got out into this area and, after leaving the highway, ran into all kinds of dust, which sifted all through the car. Then we understood why she wanted us to take water for thirst.

Once in Hagler, a dry farm community in the mountains about forty-five miles east from Rupert, Haskell and I hunted deer. We saw one, but he (the deer, not Haskell) took off over the mountain. I started the long, hard climb up after him to see if I could get a glimpse of where he went, but by the time I got to the top, the deer had disappeared.

Once Marj and I drove up to Albion in Brother Yadon's Model A Ford for a service. On the way back to Rupert that night afterwards, we saw a big sack of potatoes that had apparently dropped off a truck while somebody hauled them down the mountain. We picked up the potatoes and took them back to Brother and Sister Yadon's home. It was nip and tuck because of the Depression, and having extra people in the home put a burden on Brother and Sister Yadon. Times were difficult for the wife and me as well, so that sack of potatoes held great meaning for us then.

During this time, Wylie and Mamie Craven's little girl became very ill. They took her to a doctor in Soda Springs whom they knew quite well and in whom they had a lot of confidence. Brother and Sister Yadon had gone up to be with them. Unfortunately the little girl's appendix had ruptured and peritonitis had set in, so she passed away. Brother Yadon phoned us to let us know they were coming, so we cleaned the church as best we could for her funeral. The burial was not too far from Rupert.

Though those times could be really hard going, we certainly enjoyed our months there. The Yadons' daughter Jewel had been born when they studied in Oakland, and now they had Bud.

I remember Harry as a little baby crying and crying in his basket, chewing his fists. Marj would wonder what in the world caused him to be hungry all the time. Why did he emit that pathetic cry indicating hunger? She would give him his milk, and when she would go back into the room, the bottle would be empty and lying in the bassinet by Harry.

Marjorie and Ruth began to watch. One day they noticed Bud, who was a bit older than Harry and now walking around, watching them. After they would bring Harry the milk and leave, Bud would slip over, get the bottle, drink it dry, and lay it back in the crib. Having found out what was causing Harry to be so hungry, they worked it all out. Harry was very satisfied, and Bud was taken care of as well.

We've had a lot of fun teasing Bud Yadon these many years. He said that he did not realize until years later that we were not really blood relatives. He had always spoken of us as Uncle Ellis and Aunt Marj. There's been a close association down through the years.

Brother Yadon was true to his promise to see what he could do to help us find a place. Through him, a new work opened for us in Clarkston, Washington. Sister Eads had made contact with Brother Yadon. He didn't know too much about the church and hadn't been there himself, but he told her about us.

We were sent funds enabling us to drive our car north

to Clarkston, where we moved into a church that had belonged to a group of brethren who had divided up over a problem. One had gone off to Kamai and Winchester, Idaho. Another man, Brother Barnett, had stopped coming to church due to sheer discouragement. These two brethren had led that work. Only a few saints were left: Sister Eads, her son George (who worked in a Lewiston bank) and daughter Zella; Sister Futter and her son Cecil; a very fine old gentleman, Brother Wohld, whose son was a state patrolman for Washington, and a few others. Sister Eads paid the rent on the parsonage we lived in and helped us with other things as well. Brother Wohld would go down to the building, build a fire, then worship, get blessed of the Lord, and have a great time. Sometimes we'd arrive just before church service to find this very precious saint lying on the floor under the power of the Holy Spirit, talking in tongues and having a great time with God.

The church building wasn't too old in years, but the lath had come from green wood, so that when it dried out and shrank, it left large cracks in the plaster. This brilliant innovation had been thought out by the mill in Lewiston, Idaho.

Another problem: the land itself did not belong to the church people—they'd only leased it for a few years. Therefore, they had not been able to build on a proper foundation, but had laid the building on eight-inch-by-eight-inch cantilevers laid on the ground. It was quite a large structure, and due to not having proper air circulation, as time went by the floor dampened and began to rot. One lady's heels went through the church floor one day. That had to be patched over (the floor, not the lady).

140

This new work we endeavored to carry on as best we could to honor the Lord's name. We met a number of people there who loved the Lord, and we tried to do what we could. We remained there for a number of months visiting not only the Clarkston people but across the river in Lewiston, Idaho, as well, where some old-time saints knew God and loved Him and His cause. Many of these have, of course, passed on to their reward long since.

We invited people door to door occasionally and held special meetings, but we could not afford a major evangelistic program. Financially, we had a very difficult time. And most important, in those days we had no one to give us guidance, no one to whom we could turn other than the Lord to help us make it through.

We did all we could, in the knowledge we had then and in circumstances perhaps more than I could cope with, to stir up interest. During one time of special prayer meetings in the Clarkston church, I came down with the measles. Of course, I couldn't go to church with that, so I stayed home, but Marj went.

The PMA had changed its name to Pentecostal Church Incorporated (PCI) and had held its first conference in Nampa, Idaho, in 1931. We planned to organize the work within the framework of the Northwestern District, but no one in our congregation was suitable for church board membership—Sister Eads was a woman, her husband was a secret disciple (a fine man but not a church member), their son George was too young, Daddy Wohld was too old, and none of the others had received the Holy Spirit.

Brother Barnett, who had left the church before we came, now saw the way things were going and came back. He was the only one we knew of who could hold a position

141

of trustee or church board member. We contacted Kenneth Wine, sectional presbyter with the PCI, relative to coming over to set the church in order. He planned to come and organize the church, but during the meantime Brother Barnett received a message from his company rapidly transferring him from the Lewiston area to Tacoma. That ended our hopes of organizing the church as we had contemplated doing.

Brother Barnett had been somewhat behind in his tithing, so his family gave us some things to help make our home more comfortable and convenient—curtains, fruit. We had blinds, but couldn't afford curtains.

Then the Barnetts' time came to leave, and more of the existing support stopped as they moved away. Then one of the ladies who used to give about ten cents each Sunday moved away.

I remember Marjorie trying to bake bread. She had a hard time because the small kitchen stove had a crack in it. For heat, sometimes when we had the finances we would go over to the mill in Lewiston and buy some sawdust logs.

Eventually finances became so tight that again we couldn't buy Harry the milk he needed. Marjorie would mix a little water with the milk to help stretch it, satisfy his hunger, and sustain him. As more time went by, we couldn't drive the car because we couldn't afford gasoline, so we started walking the gravel road to church, wheeling Harry in a little cart. Then Marjorie's shoe soles went bad, and we did not have money enough to procure soles for her shoes. We put cardboard inside. And all this time, Harry didn't have the milk he should. We tried to carry on on such an extremely limited budget—nip and tuck and quite a bit of it was tuck.

Then one day a letter came from Harry Morse in Oak-land. The church had held a special function for him during which they had given him an offering. He sent nine dollars to us—half of what he had received. That meant Marjorie could have her shoes half-soled, we could buy some gas and, of course, Harry could have milk. Then, of course, those funds ran out and we were back where we'd been before. We carried on like this for some time.

One night we had a very good turnout. The city recorder from Clarkston attended. I felt impressed to tell the man sitting by the old wood stove that he might be well advised to move elsewhere because the plaster from the ceiling had cracked, looked very bad, and was hanging very low. I was afraid it might fall right on him. When he looked up and saw the situation, he very readily changed, and later in the service it did fall—with a crash.

The city recorder, there for his first and last service, the Alpha and the Omega of his visitation, sat by the center aisle several rows back. During the service he would look up toward the ceiling, then turn his head around toward the rear part of the sanctuary to follow the crack running from above the platform to the entrance of the room. I suppose the roof caused some apprehension on his part when he viewed what was above him, and I don't know if he got too much out of the service, but he was there that once, so we got a chance to minister to him.

Once George Eads's father traveled with us to Salem. We wanted to see my folks and he had to go there for some business, so he went along with us. George was the most faithful young person we had in the church. We appreciated his faithfulness during those days in Clarkston

143

and in subsequent years that he ministered with our brethren in the Northwest so loyally. Sister Eads—so very faithful—earned our gratitude.

Nevertheless, even though people were faithful, due to the lack of finances and a lot of circumstances the enumeration of which would take too long, we had to make some change. Not only did we have very little and a small baby to feed, but Marj was pregnant, so soon our financial burden would increase.

In the meantime, a letter arrived from Brother and Sister Wine requesting us to consider visiting Tieton, Washington, to let the people there have a chance to see us and to decide whether or not they would like to have us as pastor. The Wines had been there for a long time and were getting ready to go as missionaries to India.

We resigned the pastorate in Clarkston and the work closed. There was no alternative. Nowadays, when a home missionary runs out of financial help, people suggest securing gainful employment, but back in '34, you were there to work for the Lord, so you did not consider secular work. You would sink or swim, survive or perish. We perished.

I don't regret those days. We did what we could, and they helped prepare Marjorie and me for India.

Harry Scism, nine months old, around Christmas 1934, with his grandparents, Grace and John.

Harry in Tieton (1935?) at a tender age.

145

CHAPTER THIRTEEN

Tieton

hile we assisted Brother Wine in Tieton, he would make a list of things for me to do, then stand around and talk to me while I took care of these things. I was amused because I thought that since he'd made the list, he'd leave it with me and go do something else. Anyway, we did what we could to help the situation and their preparations for India. Then the people, having made up their minds, voted us in. We pastored there from 1935 to 1938.

Harry was just a little boy when we went to Tieton, and Marj gave birth to our daughter, Ferne, on September 15, 1935, in the back of the old Tieton church building. Mother Moyer helped Marjorie like a midwife. I think Sister Berry, a neighbor close by, came over also. We think Ferne got her red hair from my dad's sister.

We had a good group of people in Tieton, and after the

Wines left, the church didn't forget them. We helped send them parcels, barrels of canned fruit packed in sawdust, and so on. The people in Tieton were very good to stand by Brother and Sister Wine while they were overseas. And during our days in Tieton, we heard from the Wines in India from time to time.

Of course, all this time we did not feel inclined to forget our own desire to go to India. Rather, in the various pastorates we had, we would explain to the people that we felt called to India and that, when the time came that we could go, we would. Naturally, we did not want to keep the congregation disturbed or in a state of unrest by continually advocating our going to the mission field. At that juncture we had no idea when the door would open.

One lady in the church who was a little perturbed with me suggested that, since the Scisms were called to India, the church would do well to sponsor them and get them on the way. She offered to give a certain amount. We all laughed about this because she seemed less interested in our arriving in India than in our getting started on the way.

Meanwhile, we stayed in Tieton and pastored the nice little group there. Everything was new to us—Tieton was only my second pastorate.

One lady had a nervous breakdown. Brother Lappin and Brother Narum each prayed for her on different occasions, and she almost tore the shirt off the back of one of them. She was not delivered, and later on when we'd visit, she'd see spiders on the walls and say that devils were after her.

One day, while I sat in a chair in her living room with my big thirteen triple-A shoes sticking out in front of me, she lay in bed in her bedroom. Because of the bed's position, she could not see me, but she could see and identify my number thirteens. She asked me to come into her room to pray for her.

Marj and I canned a lot of fruit for her, since she had a large family whom she couldn't care for. Her husband did his best—we saw him rarely, as he'd attended church only for his babies' dedications.

Later, she was committed to the state mental institution at Moses Lake. They were very strict with her. One time they served her beans, and she let them know she did not like beans, but the next day she had beans again. They broke her will. Finally, they released her and returned her to her family. When she would come to church, she would cry. She wore colored glasses so that when she went home her husband would not see that she'd been crying in church. She was very tenderhearted and we thought a lot of her for that.

On a Sunday morning Ivan Berry and Opal Towell were united in marriage. As they took the vows, Opal trembled from head to foot. We have since seen them in Red Bluff, California.

Brother and Sister Sweir very faithfully attended and backed the church. Brother and Sister Henry Narum were very strong members, and we visited their home several times. Brother and Sister Christiansen were also strong members.

One lady used to tell a story about going to a basketball game in which her niece had been playing. The aunt got so happy that she lost the glasses off her face, but when she came to and saw what had happened, they were on the floor, all tromped to pieces. She used this story to illustrate how wonderful it was to be blessed of the Lord and

149

happy in Him. One time in Tieton when we had a foot-washing service, this lady really got blessed, danced, and had a great time.

Some members were not so great. One lady in a ladies' meeting pretended to receive the Holy Spirit speaking in tongues. She'd heard others. Later on, she confessed that she'd faked it. The insincerity problem is not new.

This congregation had an old building constructed out of material brought down from a camp higher in the mountains. Apparently, this sawmill town had contained little creatures known as bedbugs. We had quite a struggle with them because they were in the lumber itself. These prevalent little creatures would get into the old-fashioned opera seats we had in the sanctuary and sometimes in the bed—a general nuisance. We did everything we could—poisoned the wallpaper paste and put on heavy wallpaper, fumigated the whole building by burning sulphur—but never could really conquer this situation. In fact, nothing we did in any way seemed to decrease the size or number of these little unwelcome creatures that had come along and would do their best to disturb one's restful slumber.

One time an evangelist, Fred Ulrich, came by. He stayed in the parsonage because we had no finances to rent a motel room and no motels in Tieton then anyway. Naturally, he would stay with us. I felt I should let him know the situation, and when I told him we had the unwholesome bedbug creatures about the premises, he felt he'd best not bring all his clothes into his bedroom, but only what he would definitely need. He left the rest of his clothes in the car.

The house had two bedrooms upstairs. We had to go through two rooms on the main floor, step up on a platform on the left side, cross to the right side, then ascend a flight of stairs to the first bedroom, where Marjorie and I stayed all the time. Here we put a wood stove and here I studied. We could only get to the second bedroom through this first one—not a very convenient situation, but here guests had to stay.

A number of visiting ministers came. We had some really good services and really enjoyed our days in Tieton.

Brother Maulden, pastor in Yakima when we first went to Tieton, would come out the sixteen to eighteen miles to give some of his lectures on British Israelism, which he favored. He hadn't believed this early in life, only later on, and though he held it as a personal idea, he did not believe it as a matter of salvation.

He wasn't highly educated, but read a lot and had bettered himself, spoke with fluency, enunciated excellently, preached very well, and also was a good Bible teacher. He'd given his lectures while Brother and Sister Wine were there, and I did not feel any particular change was necessary and so suggested to him that he keep on coming, which he did. However, I noticed that it wasn't keeping up interest, so we had to make a change, and did.

We'd visit Brother Maulden's church in Yakima for fellowship meetings and special meetings. Tieton was up on The Bench near Mt. Rainier, while Yakima was a much bigger, more centrally located town.

At Yakima, various speakers would come from Canada teaching on various subjects connected with British Israelism, such as the pyramids, the measurements, and all of that. One night, after having heard one of these speakers at what they called the Women's Twentieth Century Club in the city, I stepped outside to see this man who I'd heard speaking just a few minutes before, standing there and smoking a cigarette. This let me know that he was not what, in my background, I would term a born-again Christian by any measure. We do recognize that some men merely fill certain positions in life as a matter of vocation rather than having their hearts sincerely in their ministry. We also recognize that some men have been taught differently.

Eventually, Brother Maulden resigned the pastorate in Yakima. Later, he got into British Israelism very forcefully and left the United Pentecostal fellowship. Now, many years later, he is advanced in age and not able to get out of the house much, living in Meridian, Idaho.

Since I was a bit of a retiring disposition, being elected sectional presbyter surprised me. In some sections, one person might be the only one qualified. I don't know if I was qualified or not; all I know is that I was elected. During my years of pastoring in Twin Falls and Rupert, I again served in a district board position. The district board minutes for 1931-36 were lost en route to a conference. For this book, I've been able to consult minutes going back to 1937.

Harlen Talbert became pastor of the church in Yakima. Although the previous pastor, Brother Maulden, had believed in British Israelism, one of the church brothers was very anti-British Israelism. After Brother Talbert pastored there and had perhaps not declared himself on British Israelism, this brother invited Oscar Vouga to start another church in Yakima.

Time went by, and after some weeks, quite a conflict arose in the church over Oscar Vouga starting another church in the same city of less than ten thousand, a violation of the rules we had then. Brother Vouga knew he was violating the rules, but he was also German Swiss.

Brother Talbert was a member of the PCI, so one day he came to me, since I was his sectional presbyter, with a petition. I felt it my duty to stand by Brother Talbert because he was licensed by the church and pastored the original church, so I signed the statement, though I do not recall just all it said.

W. E. Kidson, the organization's leader, came and talked to Brother Vouga. As a result Brother Kidson made it possible for Brother Vouga to take a church in Houston, Texas, and thus resolved the problem. Then Haskell Yadon came to Yakima in January 1937.

Before Brother Yadon pastored in Yakima, he held revival meetings for us in Tieton one winter. We had two stoves in the church, which kept it warm, and Brother Yadon says, "It was easy to go to sleep and my preaching was not very rousing anyway. I remember especially one brother, Brother Sweir, who always seemed to go to sleep while the preacher was preaching. One night, not only Brother Sweir, but most everybody else except two old ladies had fallen asleep. I looked around. Brother Scism and those sitting on the platform were blinking and nodding. Brother Sweir was completely out. I discovered that I was almost talking to myself. That night I wasn't too successful."

While Brother Haskell pastored in Yakima, Joe Goss, the son of Howard Goss, was with Ruth and Haskell in Yakima in services. Later on, he came to Tieton with us in special services.

Joe Goss and Allen Burgess slept in that second bedroom we had. Allen said that Brother Goss would lie in the middle of the bed and that Allen would have to put forth quite a bit of energy to raise Joe Goss's arm so that he could crawl in on his side of the bed. They would have a lot of fun teasing one another. One service, Brother Goss wanted Marjorie to play her guitar while he sang, which she did.

Sometimes all of us ministers got together. Once Brother Hurt scheduled a harvest festival. Bill and Alice Nigh, who pastored in Ellensburg, came by, and since they had a nice car compared to my jalopy, we rode with them. Alice Nigh played the piano well and they sang together. On that enjoyable journey a quartet of us sang a song to the whole group regarding the "stone hewn out of the mountain." Someone had placed a Bible where it would be found later on, so we went around here and there, looking for the stone hewn out of the mountain. Finally, we found the stone, so all arrived together in one place and sang that we had found the stone hewn out of the mountain. It was—different.

J. A. Johnson, Joe Goss, Haskell Yadon, and I comprised that quartet. I never could add anything to a quartet, but that was the way it went.

Meanwhile, we had some very fruitful days in Tieton, which we enjoyed so very much. The church grew.

Dad came down with sciatica rheumatism. His muscles would contract, and I saw him suffer.

Then Mother came down with illness. She had diabetes and perhaps some traces of the lung cancer that took her later. We didn't know all this at first, and they did not have insulin as we have today, so she would break out with spots on her feet or limbs and suffer so much. Mother and Dad requested us to come home and help them, so we did, and cheerfully. Since we had a church, I had to take leave of absence, and did in 1936. I left Clinton Brown to supply for me, and we went home with our children, Harry and Ferne. Harry was just a little boy, and Ferne was a baby.

Marjorie, Harry, Ferne, and I moved from Tieton to Salem, where I obtained employment with the city. My dad's second cousin had been his boss, so when Dad could no longer work, Dad's cousin put in a good word for me. Dad also talked to them about my coming. They all, including the engineer, knew why I had returned home.

After getting settled in, one day I went down to the city barns, where I met Hugh Rogers, the engineer, the head honcho, who happened to be there. I told him I needed a job. he said, "Let me see your hands." When I opened my hands and showed them to him, he said, "They look mighty white to me." I said, "Well, they would become calloused in time," and, of course, that's how things turned out.

I worked for the city of Salem all the time we stayed there. Each work day started at 7:00 AM, and much of it was digging ditches for sewer pipe and cleaning out sewer lines; some was putting in curbs and streets, repairing concrete, patching holes in streets and sidewalks, repairing bridges, grading, and leveling. In those days it was mostly by hand, not at all as it is now when things are so highly mechanized.

On one of our assignments, Ray and I worked with others breaking up and moving an old concrete steel bridge. Earlier I had almost lost my life at this bridge. The bridge itself was not too long—it crossed Mill Creek due to flash floods. However, the heavy rains had flooded the creek, washing away the pea gravel under the bridge and causing the main bridge to sink. The city sent me with planks eighteen to twenty feet long and three inches by twelve inches. I laid those on the main part of the bridge, stood with one foot on each, and locked an air-driven, 185-pound jackhammer between my knees. I hammered two spots into the bridge skirting when suddenly the skirting cracked, gave way, and fell into the river. As the water rushed beneath and around me, I threw out my arms to the two planks I was standing on. The air hose and jack-hammer were caught under the fallen skirting. I was able to pull up my body to an upright position with what strength I had. One of the bystanders said he had thought they'd have to go in and pull me out.

In the summer after the creek had dried to a trickle, we were sent back to break up the bridge. At that time, two little boys with a wagon found the jackhammer lying in the creek. They packed it on, hoping to sell it to an Italian who ran a wrecking yard, but a bystander saw them take it and told them it belonged to the city, so they should take it there, which they did.

When we broke up the bridge and cleared away the debris, Ray and I tried to move steel-reinforced concrete blocks. We'd roll them onto a big wooden platform, then they'd crane them up to big trucks at the street level. While rolling these big concrete blocks, I suggested to Ray that if he gave a big puff on his strong-smelling cigar, he could roll the block right onto the platform. He wasn't very happy—more touchy in those days. He's mellowed a lot.

We had regular shovels and spades with bevelled blades five inches wide and twelve to fourteen inches long with which we'd dig our ditches. We had to try to keep the ditch even as we went down. Sometimes the ditch was so deep that I would shovel dirt up onto a platform halfway up the ditch wall, and another man would shovel the dirt from there to the ground above.

Naturally, we worked in Oregon's weather—once in rain-repellent gear for twenty-one consecutive days.

When the soil was sandy or pea gravel or otherwise inclined to cause a fill-in, we would install legging (planks boarded up against the ditch walls and jacked or braced in place, tightened by means of a screw to keep the soft or sandy soil or pea gravel from falling in on us while we were down so deep in the ground). Each person would dig a distance of twenty to twenty-five feet.

While laying pipes, we had to make sure they lay at a proper gradient in order for the water and whatnot to flow through without becoming stopped up, whether the pipe or its contents were deep or shallow.

I worked in Salem about a year. During this time, Weston Howard, a cousin who had lived in our neighborhood during my boyhood and who now worked in southern Oregon, crawled under a Caterpillar tractor to do some needed repair work. Somehow, the Caterpillar fell on him and he lost his life. Ike Scism, another cousin, came and told me about Weston, asking if I would take the graveside service. Ike contacted his sister (Weston's widow) and some others connected with the family, and we had the graveside service.

Eventually and slowly, Dad's health improved and he was able to work again. He felt much better, but physically he was never the same. He went back to work, but he was bent forward, and the disease affected him the rest of his life.

Mother's health remained much the same. Marj and I returned to Tieton and resumed our pastoral endeavor. Clinton Brown was a bit hesitant to give up the pastorate, but otherwise amenable. He knew why we had left and why we had returned.

Most of the Tieton people raised apples of one variety or another—Delicious, Roman Beauties, Jonathans. There's wonderful orchard country all through there. Migrant workers would come to pick the beautiful apples in the region.

The apple trees there lean mostly in one direction. They say that Tieton was named one day when a man's hat blew off and someone yelled at him to "tie it on."

For good apples, you need hot days, cool nights, and lots of spring. One year, an early freeze wiped out much of the apple crop, which hit hard the people who had orchards. But the union warehouse really incensed people because, when they sold their fruit to the union warehouse, the union authorities piled up all the apples that had fly stings, and so on that wouldn't sell for the best price, and poured kerosene on them to keep people from eating them and not buying union products. This disturbed some of us a great deal because poor people who followed the harvest around the country couldn't benefit from this fruit that had been mostly edible.

Naturally, everyone looked forward to apple harvest in the fall. In those days of very difficult finances, when the situation was nip and tuck, the tuck was usually closer. Many poor people received free food from the government; they also very conscientiously did all they could to help— much more so than often took place in later years.

In the fall of each year, we would put apples down on

the ground in a little dugout underneath the platform. Sometimes we kept vegetables down there, too, as people gave them. Many vegetables might not have been first class, and might have a worm sting or maybe more, but other than that they were good eating and we enjoyed them. They helped us.

During those difficult, Depression days, many church people not in the apple business worked for the Public Works Administration. One time when we drove down from the bluff to the church pastored by Bill Austin in Natchez, Washington, a small town five or more miles away by the Natchez River, we saw one of the Public Works Administration employees sitting on a square shovel and another man pulling him along on the snow. This appealed to Harry, just a little fellow then, so he decided that when he became older he would like to work with the Public Works Administration. We would tease him a great deal later about his ambitions.

Sometimes when we'd go to Natchez, Sister Sweir would go with us. There, Howard West and his brothers would camp in tents along the river. Years later, Howard married her daughter, Helen Marie Sweir, and pastored in New Westminster, British Columbia, Canada, and in Idaho.

Our children grew in the church. One day Marj and I came from the parsonage to the sanctuary in time to see Harry in front of everyone, showing off his sister, Ferne. He was so proud of her.

Ferne had her own way of introducing herself. When she was maybe two years old and the preachers, especially some of the younger ones, would tease her, she would become rather disturbed at their activity at her expense, and since her only way to get back was to bite, she became afflicted with this habit. As a result, she picked up some sort of disease and we had to take her to the doctor down below the bluff along the Natchez River.

She would sit on the front seat in church. We had taught the young people not to hold Harry and Ferne after they became old enough to sit up by themselves.

During a particular fellowship meeting, while Mother Pierce was speaking, Ferne stood up. I motioned to her to sit down. I could not hear what she said, but I could tell by the formation of her lips that she was saying no. There was no way I could get down unobtrusively—in those days, one had to depart the platform by walking from where Marjorie and I sat playing the trumpet and guitar, across the platform, then down the side steps—yet we had taught our children to obey.

Later in the meeting, Ferne finally sat down, then later still again got off her seat and stood on the floor. I went through the same procedure and she through hers. Then I was able to leave the platform, and though the church was crowded, I felt this was necessary. I picked her up in my arms and started for the vestibule. As we disappeared, she cried out, "Daddy, don't pank, don't pank." Of course, we then went through another little procedure on that occasion, but generally we had very little trouble with the kids.

One time Harry was doing something I felt he shouldn't have engaged in, so I started a chorus, walked down from the platform, and took care of that situation. Little things did come along.

Once when Haskell Yadon held a meeting in Tieton, Ferne was still a baby, but Harry was big enough to carry in some wood. Haskell watched him go outside, get an armload, come in, unload it into the woodbox near the stove, then take his hat off, walk out, and put it back on. We'd taught Harry that men don't wear hats indoors, but he couldn't take it off as soon as he came in because his arms were full of wood.

We had times of recreation, especially getting out in the snow whenever we could. One time while my brother and his wife, Maybelle, lived in Yakima, they came out to Tieton for a visit.

An old gentleman in the Tieton church, Brother Snyder, who used to carry mail on snow shoes and skis in Idaho, told Ray that when he carried mail on skis, he would gain quite a bit of speed on downhill grades. He would pile gunny sacks over a pole, hold the pole between his legs, then draw up on it, pressing against it with his legs, to slow himself down when he was descending a long slope. Ray decided to do the same thing, but used an apple prop (a long two-inch-by-two-inch board for supporting sagging apple orchard tree limbs)—not cylindrical at all and far too long. He put on skis, sat down on the gunny sack, really bent it, and started down a slope on a hill out of Tieton. His skis went one way and he went another, so we had quite a bit of excitement.

On another trip, we built a toboggan out of wood, less than a foot wide, but six to eight feet long. We cut the wood and constructed a bow on the toboggan, nose up, and nailed tin to it. Then with a hot iron we affixed paraffin to the bottom to make it plenty slick to slide along smoothly. We couldn't guide it much, however. You should have seen some of the scrapes we got into.

One time we built a mound of snow on the side of a hill. We'd go over that and on down. Toward the bottom was an irrigation canal. Ray lay down on the toboggan with a pocket watch in his pocket. When he went over the little jump we had there for the toboggan to land on, his body slammed down onto the watch and toboggan, ruining his pocket watch.

Another time, three or four young folks were on a toboggan when the snow had frozen and crusted. They came up with some scarred faces, especially Lee Shutt, because those in the rear had pushed him (he was in front) into the frozen snow. It had scratched his face quite badly.

One time Haskell Yadon and I were out together and went over one of these jumps. It caught me in a twist, and when I landed at the bottom, I could not get my breath. I don't know exactly what happened. This was how we had exercise during the winter.

In Salem I purchased an Oakland car. In 1937, we left it with Brother Yadon in Yakima and borrowed his car to take a couple of young ladies to Oakland, California, to Harry Morse's missionary training home. On our way there, his throw-out bearing on the drive shaft went bad. We had to return to Yakima, have that repaired, then set out again.

We spent several days in Oakland visiting the Morses, then went down to Exeter for the California PCI conference.

Eventually the time came when Marj and I felt we should make a change. Meanwhile, the church in Twin Falls invited us to see if we and they wanted us to pastor there. We borrowed Haskell's car and went to Twin Falls, staying for a couple of weeks with Annie Hills. Brother Ludlow, an elder in the church, was taking care of the con-

162

gregation between pastors. The church voted. We accepted, and prepared to move to Twin Falls.

PCI district conference, August 11-13, 1936. Front row, left to right: Emmanuel Rohn, J. A. Johnson, Kenneth Wine, Alonzo Saunders, J. S. Frederick (of Sulphur, LA), Ernest Wine, Haskell Yadon. Ladies' row: Sis. J. A. Johnson, Dorothy Yadon (Paul Yadon's wife), unknown, Hellen Belden in front, Ruth Sweeten in back, Helen Nordby, unknown, Sister Wilson (gray hair), Brother Jenkin's mother (?), Sister Warner (?), Ruth Yadon. Top row: Ernest Howell, S. C. Curry, Paul Yadon, Harlan Talbert, Sister Talbert (?), Peter Jenkins, Archie Stone (with the bus), Frank Lowe (I traded my Hudson to him and he gave me his beat-up Ford), unknown (I preached the funeral for his wife in Corvallis; at another time he testified about Jesus being "gooder and gooder." When he added that it was good to know who Jesus is, the Assemblies of God lady chairing the meeting called him "Jesus only"), Bob Sweeten, Ellis Scism.

Ellis and Harry during Tieton days (1935-38)

CHAPTER FOURTEEN

Twin Falls—The Saints and the Conference

*I*n 1938, we left Tieton and took the church in Twin Falls, Idaho, first probably in May to check the situation. Later in the year, we moved to Twin Falls, and Bob Sweeten followed me in Tieton. Later, he followed me in Rupert, Idaho, too.

After we had gone to Twin Falls, we had to travel back to Tieton to collect some fruit that Marjorie had canned but that we had not been able to haul in the trailer the first time. The car broke down on our way from Idaho to Washington, so we had quite a trip. This delayed our journey for some time, but we made it for the conference.

During that visit to Tieton, a wedding took place. Marion Fretwell and Pearl Snyder had planned a wedding, and Pearl had borrowed Marjorie's veil for the occasion. When I was pastor and they had known I was leaving, they asked me to perform the ceremony. I had declined and informed them that the matter should be taken care of by the pastor they would have at the time. Due to the car being broken down, I was there while the wedding would take place. Again they asked me and again I told them how I felt. I offered my services to Brother Sweeten to assist however I could on this occasion. I learned later that this was Brother Sweeten's first wedding. He borrowed my black tie to perform the ceremony in. I was glad things worked out as they did.

We took on the responsibilities of our pastorate in Twin Falls and held jail services. Every Sunday we went, the boys wanted three favorite songs sung: "When the Roll is Called Up Yonder," "The Old Rugged Cross," and "In the Garden." These same songs that appealed to them we also enjoyed very much during our time spent at the Twin Falls County Jail.

We also held county poor farm services on Sunday afternoons. The county ran and paid for these, to benefit the infirm and needy. This was not a workhouse, just a place to care for people who needed help. We might as well help—we never knew if we'd be next.

These services, both at the jail and at the poor farm, led me into contact with the county sheriff. He later told me that he wanted me to meet a man who had lost his reason and been brought from Buhl to the Twin Falls County Jail. Authorities from the state asylum planned to come and get him. I went over there and they let me into his steel tank—solid steel walls. He was wearing bib overalls and a work shirt. This fellow told me that he didn't know just what he could do for me, but that if he could help me in any way, to let him know. During my visit, the authorities from the state asylum escorted him downstairs, all the while the deputy sheriffs keeping a close watch on him. Near the elevator, he made a break for it. They ran and grabbed him, then took him off to the state asylum.

Marjorie and Gladys Hills held children's services. I remember an outstanding result concerning an inveterate smoker's little girl, who was quite the sunshine in his home—she would want them to pray and ask God's blessing at mealtime and so on. One day when her mother stepped out of the house for some reason, she was playing near the stove. Her dress caught on fire, which resulted ultimately in her death. The following Sunday as we had the funeral service, her father repented. He took out his cigarettes, laid them on the platform we used for an altar, and gave his heart to God.

This performed a wonderful change in his life from that time forward. We have lost track of them during the many years since then, but it was an outstanding result of the children's services.

The Twin Falls First Pentecostal Church had wonderful people. Charlie Yadon, a teenager there, worked in Rock Creek Canyon, where his parents lived. He greatly helped me in anything he could do around the church, except one time when I suggested to him that he crawl underneath the platform through an opening door behind the church. He didn't want to do this because the spiders had assiduously woven their webs there. In Twin Falls, we had the very poisonous black widow spider. He declined my offer.

Another time, he traveled with John Calder to a camp meeting in Bend, Oregon. They spent one night in the mountains. Charlie Yadon said he would sleep in his sleeping bag outside the tent. During the night, he heard some very unusual noises. Later, John Calder told me that

Charlie, without getting out of the sleeping bag, had just humped his way over to the tent so that his head was inside the tent flap while the rest of his body remained outside.

A few months later, he went to A. D. Hurt's Bible college in Boise and met his future wife there.

One time when the Northwestern District camp meeting was to be held in Parma, Idaho, the tent and poles were piled on the ground, and Charlie Yadon offered to watch the stuff that night. Some of the young people in the Parma church knew that Charlie was a bit apprehensive in the dark, so they dressed up. After dark, they slowly approached and whispered loud enough for him to hear. Finally, they said, "Let's rush him." Charlie took a side pole with an iron piece coming out the end and started whirling it around his head. They knew they'd really scared him, so they had a good laugh.

Charlie had a good ministry, became one of our good preachers, and had very many good meetings. One time during his Cascade, Idaho, revival meetings he wanted the people to respond and come to the altar. I passed through there and he commented to me that he wondered if he jumped over the pulpit, maybe people would respond. This of course indicated his zeal. I told him that I did not think this was the key. He didn't jump over the pulpit, but he had good services anyway. Later, he went to Alaska as an evangelist.

I saw Charlie from time to time in conferences, and so on. Ultimately he married Orphah Marshall, a nice person. They lived with her parents in Washington. She passed away with cancer while they pastored in Vancouver, Washington, for a number of years. He was superintendent of

Washington District and is now an honorary member of the United Pentecostal Church General Board. He remarried and pastored in Puyallup, Washington. He is now pastor emeritus.

Another young man in the Twin Falls church, Oliver Brown, would stand on the high platform in the old First Pentecostal Church, play his guitar, and sing songs of the Crawford Family (they sang a lot on the radio). Later, Oliver was inducted into the Navy in World War II. I've seen him since, but not for many years, and have now lost track of him.

Frank Yadon would stand beside Oliver with his hat on his head (before he received the Holy Ghost) and accompany him on the violin. Strangers would sometimes say, "What's wrong with that man? Why doesn't he take his hat off in church?" I would explain that all our people knew that if anyone ever said anything to him, he'd never darken the church doors again. Out of deference, we refrained from any untoward comment that would cause him to feel unwelcome or that we questioned his behavior.

Frank had no hair, eyebrows, or eyelashes. He'd had a fever as a little boy, lost all his hair, and none of it had ever grown back. He was extremely self-conscious about his baldness.

During meetings with Oscar Vouga, one night Frankie came with a new hat and suit into the prayer room. As he knelt to pray, he did not remove his new hat. While on his knees, he fell over backward under the power of God. His hat rolled on its brim across the prayer room. Then he began speaking in other tongues as the Spirit of God gave utterance.

It was a marvelous deliverance. After that, I saw him

169

coming into church during harvest festival and taking his hat off like anyone else. Later, at the harvest festival in Boise, when the Spirit of God came on him, he'd jump maybe three feet high, and that bald head of his would shine like a light.

God had really done a wonderful work in his life, breaking up the inferiority complex that had so bothered him for years. This real miracle of God's grace very triumphantly portrayed God's ability and power to break the bondage that can hamper and engross and surround life.

The Holy Ghost renewed Frank's life. I saw this wonderful boy inducted into the service for World War II. I went with his father to the draft board to see if Frank could possibly be deferred, but they made it clear that there was no way, so Frank went on.

When haircut day came at Farragut, Idaho, Frank didn't have any hair to cut. In the army, as I understand, you're just a number. When his number came, he just waved and went on. He had a very good spirit about it all, and we rejoiced in the beautiful understanding of the direct miracle God had performed in his life.

As time went by, the subject came up of Frank's getting married. His nephew, Emmet's boy, went to his grandfather one day and said, "Grandpa, do you have fifty dollars to loan Shank to get married?" ("Shank" was Frank's nickname.) When his grandad said no, Emmet's boy said, "Well, it isn't every girl that would marry a man without any hair on his head." Frank had been seeing Ida, who later became his wife, and had commented that if he had fifty dollars he would get married, hence Emmet's son's concern for his Uncle Shank.

Later, Frank and Ida moved to the coast, and while we

were on one of our deputation trips through Washington after we'd been in India, we saw Frank and Ida in the Tacoma area. Frank was working on a farm, harrowing in the dust, his eyes all red because he had no natural protection—no lashes—to keep the dust out. Later, Ida was killed in an automobile accident, and Frank moved to Alaska and became a carpenter there.

Another man in the church, Brother Newcomb, was trying to put a bulb in a car when he injured his right hand. A piece of glass had sheared off and was still caught in the upper part of the frame. While he tried to put the bulb in underneath that piece of glass, it dropped out and severed some of his tendons. Of course, he came by the parsonage for prayer with his hand all wrapped up in a towel and bloody. We prayed, then he went to the hospital. When they put the leaders back together again, the operation shortened them, leaving his thumb in an improper position.

Time went by, and later he began to work on a farm in the south under a boss with whom he had some trouble. Because of his thumb operation, he could not defend himself as he would have liked to.

I had just come back from uptown, where I'd bought a pair of gloves because in those days the parsonage had a coal furnace and one would become dirty shoveling coal into the furnace. When I came back to the parsonage, Brother Newcomb was standing there with his back toward me. I had been used to teasing him a little bit, so I just took off my gloves, gave them a toss, and hit him in the back. When I did this, he turned around, looked at me, and said I should be careful because, "You can never tell what a man will look like until you look at him face to

171

face." Sure enough, he had bruises on his face. I didn't know what in the world had happened, but I found out. Of course, he had lost his job.

After Brother Newcomb had this problem with his boss, Arthur Hills came to me one day and asked, "Brother Scism, who is going to lead the song service now?" Of course, we had to make a change. Brother Newcomb had to sit in the congregation for a while. Later on, things worked out beautifully again.

Later, Brother Newcomb, one of the two people I used in leading the song service, felt that I was not using him enough and noised this among the church people. Mother Yadon told him that if he would go into the prayer room, there was always room there. It wasn't that he'd never gone—he had from time to time, but not as I felt he should if he were to lead in worship. I observed that he heeded Mother Yadon and devoted more time to praying. After this, I felt that he should have a chance to help lead song service.

The Newcombs were very good to us. They did not have means, but they would do all they could and bring whatever they might have—cream, eggs, whatever. This we appreciated very much. Ultimately, they moved to Washington State, and I've seen them many times since.

Isabel Hills also was a great help to us, especially in leading song service—not always, but often. Later, she and Charles Albert met, presumably in Caldwell, Idaho, while in Bible school. The time came when she felt she had to make a change, which she did. She and Charles Albert started a church. When we were getting ready to leave for India in 1948, they were in Red Bluff in a little trailer home and we stopped to see them.

Harlen Talbert, who'd pastored in Yakima, later came to Twin Falls as a carpenter working on a Japanese camp. There he attended the church I pastored and for a time stayed with us. He drove to and from his job from our house

The internment camp was out in the midst of dust and sagebrush. One day when Brother Talbert went to work, one of the other carpenters told him they were going to build a hotel there, too, so Brother Talbert asked him, "What for?"

The carpenter said, "To house the rumors." During wartime, rumors of war ran rampant.

The paranoia about Japanese-Americans affected the church. Brother June Nukida, an American-born Japanese from Idaho, had given his heart to the Lord in Parma, Idaho, and now suffered a great deal during the war days, especially when the government passed a rule that Japanese people were not allowed within so many miles of the coastal area. He traveled to our conference in Bend, Oregon, one year, then had to go back to Idaho, because the government officials refused to let him stay in Bend. In fact, they told him they could not guarantee his safety while driving back to Idaho, and I felt very bad about this.

Later he studied at Apostolic Bible Institute in St. Paul, Minnesota, then had meetings in Pocatello, Houston, San Antonio, Fresno, Manteca, and Oakland. There he married an American-born Japanese student from Western Apostolic Bible College (now Christian Life College), then went to Japan to labor as a missionary among his own people, where his American wife died. Later he married a Japanese lady there, and we met them in 1962 in Chigasaki at the annual conference, by which time he was living in Hokkaido and was the superintendent of the UPC in Japan. He gave me, as a token of friendship, a bear's head that I still have, made from Hokkaido-area wood, very beautifully carved and very appealing to the eye. It hung on our wall in Portland until after Marjorie's death and my moving back to live with Harry and Audrene in St. Louis.

Eventually, Brother Nukida moved back to America and had to live here five years before his wife could obtain American citizenship. By then, America was more hospitable to its Japanese citizens.

Brother Nukida served the Lord faithfully for many years. He passed away at about eighty-five years of age.

Later, the Talberts wanted to go to India. They applied, but never went. The missionary board, I understand, had planned to send them before Marjorie and I went. In the meantime, the merger took place in 1945, and Brother and Sister Talbert, for whatever reason, left the fellowship, so Marj and I went on without them.

While Brother Talbert was still in our fellowship, he pastored a church in El Paso. While there, he went to a fellowship meeting where he was supposed to speak. Apparently, a number of black people attended, so a well-known black preacher came, and Brother Talbert declined in favor of the black brother. During the service, whoever was in charge asked Brother Talbert to say something just before the new preacher was to speak. After Brother Talbert ended, the second man went ahead with his message after first commenting, "Let us all sing a song and get our minds collected," inferring that whatever Brother Talbert had said had so scattered the minds of the people that they needed to be shepherded back together again. At least that's the way Brother Talbert took it.

Later on, he lived in Boise and I met him many times again before he passed away.

When we hadn't pastored in Twin Falls too long and still lived in the first house, I drove with Marjorie to Bend for the district conference and camp meeting. On this visit, Marj and I took one of the girls, Irene Huff, from the Twin Falls church. We dropped Irene off with her friends in Bend, then went on to Oregon City to visit Mother Moyer before the conference was to begin.

While we visited Mother Moyer, Marjorie became very ill with a gall bladder problem. I had to attend the conference, so I left Marjorie and the children with her mother in Oregon City and went back to Bend.

After the conference, Marjorie couldn't travel, and at the same time, since Irene had helped buy gas for the car, we had an obligation to take her back to Twin Falls. The people who had come from Twin had no room in their cars for another passenger. On the other hand, I did not want anything that would bring any reproach upon my ministry or my life. Another problem was that a young man had drowned in Snake River Canyon, and I had to leave the conference early in order to preach his funeral in Twin Falls.

I had also received a telegram from Oregon City telling me to come there because Marjorie was not expected to live. All this greatly upset me. Meanwhile, the old Plymouth car was not working as it should. After my considerable effort in trying to see that everything was all right, one of the families in the church, Brother and Sister Madsen, came to my rescue, and even though they therefore couldn't stay for the whole conference, followed behind us in their one-seated car from Bend to Twin Falls.

175

After I reached Twin and dropped Irene off, since the car didn't work and I had no money to travel on, I did not know what to do, which way to turn, or how things would come out. Fortunately when I called Oregon City, I found out that Marjorie had a turn for the better and everything worked out all right.

A Dr. White had come from McMinnville to the house in Oregon City and had told Mother Moyer that, since Marjorie was so seriously ill, he might lose his patient in spite of whatever he would do, but that he had a method of manipulation supposed to clear the gall bladder of all the things that accumulate there. I've never heard of anyone since that does this type of manipulation, but in her case it turned out all right.

During all this, Arthur Hills and Charlie Yadon stayed with me. One Saturday night, we had an open-air meeting uptown. At these well-attended street services, Gladys Hills played the accordion. Two total strangers, a certain woman and her son, stood up and testified. They looked rather ragged and perhaps mildly retarded. After the meeting, they asked for the pastor. I knew they wanted me to provide food and a place to stay while they were there. Of course, with Marjorie being ill and in Oregon, I could not see how I could arrange anything feasible. Besides, they had just barged into the street meeting and started speaking without being invited, so they seemed to be the sort of people you didn't feel like helping. Therefore, Arthur Hills, Charlie Yadon, and I went for a walk and escaped that situation.

The funeral for the young man who had died in Snake River Canyon was held at the mortuary chapel in Twin Falls. A large crowd attended, very common for this type of death. The funeral hall filled up.

Brother Woods, father of the boy who had died, had previously attended B. M. David's Pentecostal Assemblies of Jesus Christ (PAJC) church, also located in Twin Falls, but he now attended First Pentecostal, so he asked me to conduct the funeral. Pastor B. M. David also came, along with Earl Klontz, a tall, big man who attended the church he pastored. Brother L., who also came, until recently had attended B. M. David's church. Brother L. had a large family—Brother B. M. David had said that if everyone else in his church left and only Brother L.'s family showed up, he'd still have a Sunday school, but just now Brother L.'s family had transferred instead to First Pentecostal.

On this hot summer day, apparently Brother L. had been having fellowship with some of his old friends who shared his Russian descent. Apparently their fellowship had included a little drinking. On this hot day, many people stood in their summer apparel in the crowd. While I spoke, I heard someone saying, "Amen" and giving similar expressions, but they did not register favorably with me. I sensed something wrong, but did not know just where or from whom it came, yet making comments about it would have been out of keeping with a funeral service. After the service ended and we went to the gravesite, I learned that the source of the remarks was Brother L.

After the internment service, B. M. David and Earl Klontz went to Brother L.'s house. By that time, because of the warmth, Brother L.'s stomach was upset and he had vomited on his shoes. He was hosing his shoes off when he saw his former pastor and Earl Klontz coming. Although he had just been out of that church for a few days, he turned the hose on his former pastor. Whether he ever reached him or not I don't know, but one of Brother L.'s sons shut the water off at the tap. This quite exciting situation naturally caused a bit of a stir in our church, and one of our brethren in particular was rather apprehensive as to what the future might hold and what part Brother L. might be permitted to play as a member of the church. Brother L. overcame this one-time liquor problem and the whole situation worked out all right, but not before it created an atmosphere of excitement, concern, and unrest during the funeral that day.

Eventually Marjorie's health improved, and I brought her back from Oregon City to Twin Falls. She had had a considerable number of gall bladder attacks before and had been very ill with them.

A man who lived next door to the church was very unhappy about our loud praying and meetings at night, especially during the later hours, so he created no little amount of trouble for the church with his complaints to the city superintendent of police. This in turn necessitated our appearing before Mr. Gillette, chief of police, at the police station.

Before I had come and while Brother Ludlow led services, the church had some really good meetings during which the Lord had blessed. Someone had come under God's power and had created a lot of noise, disturbing the man next door. He had called the police, who came and told Brother Ludlow to make this person stop. Brother Ludlow, from what I was told later, informed the policeman that he wouldn't say anything—the man was under God's power and he, Brother Ludlow, would make no effort to quench the Spirit's moving in this particular individual's life. If the policeman wanted to make him stop speaking or exalting the Lord, that was up to him. Of course, the policeman didn't want anything to do with it either, so he did not go in.

The complaints continued after I arrived, and so we talked with the police chief. We informed him that at times we could from the parsonage (the second rented place that we lived in) hear lots of noise late at night from the diamonds where people played baseball under floodlights. This naturally disturbed our sleep. He replied that if people complained because of the late, noisy baseball games, they would take action. In the meantime, we had to muffle our noise, so we installed a separate inner wooden wall in our church basement prayer room, with sawdust between the walls to soundproof it so that we would not disturb our neighbor.

In addition to all the other services, including special visits by evangelists, we had missionary services, including one with George and Helen White, veteran missionaries even then to Indonesia. During this meeting, George White said he wished Americans could see him in a village, standing out in the monsoon weather in the mud without any shoes on, pants rolled up and mud oozing between his toes, preaching the gospel message to people who had not had a chance to hear or to understand.

We hadn't lost our missionary call, and, in fact, I attended the 1940 PCI general conference in Jackson, Tennessee, for the purpose of receiving endorsement as missionaries to India. Marj couldn't come because she had to take care of the church and the kids, who were in school by this time. Our family received the endorsement, but we would not leave for India for another nine long years. All together, we'd had a call for fourteen years before deputation began in 1948.

As I look back in retrospect, I think of experiences I had that I never would have had if I'd gone out in the early days. We would have been too fresh, too new, too young to enter the mission field unprepared. Of course, we never had the particular experiences that we experienced in India, but our work in the organization helped us.

At that conference, the leaders had all the evangelists come up in front so that the pastors could see them, which was a perfectly legitimate thing to do, and Brother Coulon came up with the rest of the evangelists. Standing there, he said later, reminded him of an auction: "Who'll take him? Who'll take him?"

In later years, Brother Goss introduced him as "the man that signs follow." Brother Coulon would paint signs—a sign for your church or a motto to hang in your home. Brother Goss did not come across as being disrespectful, but unfortunately Brother Coulon took exception to his statement because he wanted to be introduced as an evangelist or Bible teacher, and not just relegated to the position of "a man that signs followed."

At this same conference, an eighteen-year-old former baseball player and then evangelist, Kenneth Reeves, met me and today still says that Ellis Scism, "so tall, Indian tall," impressed him very much. These kind and typically generous words of his I appreciate greatly, as well as the wonderful way his whole congregation treats me when I can visit.

I would keep some young men around the Twin Falls church and parsonage now and then to help encourage them as they started in God's work, and I've never felt bad about doing what I could. I gave Carl Adams his second revival. Another young man, Arthur Egbert, stayed with us in Twin Falls for a long time. He is no longer with us now, but that's not our fault—he went that way on his own.

But back then during World War II, while he was with us and aspiring to the ministry, I was asked to see whether or not my blood type matched Lois Calder's. Her husband, Allan, was in the service, and she had just given birth to a little girl and needed blood, so I went with Arthur Egbert to have our blood typed. Both types fit her need. I went first. They laid me on a table, stretched my left arm out, and began to draw the blood through a needle and little rubber syringe into a glass jar. I didn't understand all the procedure then, nor do I now for that matter, but while they were pressing the syringe, suddenly something broke—probably the glass tube inside the jar. I had been lying there watching it and feeling comfortable, but when this happened blood began to spurt out of my arm and drop down on the floor. I had been lying on a table and doing all right, watching it all, but then I began to turn woozy—I didn't pass out, but I no longer felt comfortable. Of course, the nurse ran and brought towels to soak up the blood. He finally finished drawing the needed blood, then went to Lois Calder's room in another part of the hospital.

By this time, I felt rather faint, so they tilted up the foot of the table to help blood rush to my head. I lay there for a while.

When I went back home, I told the story about all the trouble I'd had, painting a rather dark picture for the benefit of this six-foot young man who planned to go the following day to give his blood. He worried a bit, but nonetheless went and had no trouble—everything went along just fine.

181

Later, I went to meet Allan, Lois's husband, at the railway station at Gooding, and brought him about thirty miles back to Twin Falls.

In India one day, I told the Bible college students and perhaps too vividly described this incident. One of the young men passed out and some other students packed him over to a room on the mission compound property. Before too long, he came around, but apparently he was overly sensitive to hearing stories of that nature.

Meanwhile, I had presbyter duties in my new section. Quite some time after Arthur Johnson had gone to Rupert to pastor the church there, a problem arose because of a totally unfounded rumor concerning him. He had blessed me tremendously in Oakland when I was just starting out; I had been enriched by his life, his example, and ministry. But after he came to Rupert, one couple, especially a woman whose mind, it was eventually determined, had begun to slip, made some very outlandish comments regarding Brother Johnson.

He came to see me because the church was going to hold a special meeting. One of the local church board members had picked up on the comments and stood up for the woman in the midst of everything. Since I was the district official, and because Brother Johnson felt that the other brother would try to take advantage of the business meeting, he wanted me to come and preside. For ninety running hours he'd had hiccups—even while visiting Marjorie and me in Twin Falls—because he was so bothered, unnerved, and disturbed over the problem after he'd been so honorable through the years. I told him I certainly would come. We made it a point to be there, and within the confines of the organization bylaws, I presided, which precluded the possibility of the other brother presiding. As it turned out, Brother Johnson was totally exonerated. His faithful wife stood by him before, during, and after the whole crisis.

During the war days, one of the young men who used to come to church once in a great while (his father came quite faithfully) was inducted into the service and sent to an induction center some distance away. Not long after he had left, one morning, lo and behold!, he showed up at the parsonage.

I was surprised when I went to the door and invited him to come in, and still more surprised to learn that he had been AWOL. The shock of induction had perhaps so numbed him with fear that he had not considered the outcome of being AWOL. I warned him that he was subject to the penitentiary offense—I'd seen such soldiers on trains, five or six all linked together with a cable. Then he went to his home in a small adjoining town, where his parents, after duly considering the import of the situation and what would happen to him if he did not return, induced him to return. He later gave his life in Iwo Jima fighting the Japanese, so he died an honorable death for his country.

Nowadays, people might say that he would have been better off in the penitentiary than dying in Iwo Jima, but back then, before all the anti–Vietnam war feeling, personal honor and loyalty to the flag were feelings more frequently felt.

On another occasion, Harold Norton, who had been in a penitentiary or correction center of some kind in Missouri, came to stay with us. Gordon Hills, uncle of Arthur Hills, signed his papers. He came out to Idaho through the intervention of Sister Pike, who had known him somewhere along the line, and got a job working in a Twin Falls bakery. One day, some sugar or whatever spilled on the floor. This young man saw the bakery proprietor sweep it up and into a chocolate cake. Since the cake was brown anyway, people would never know the difference. Apparently one was to learn little tricks to the trade as one endeavored to enter honest society.

Elsie Allen, who later married Frank Yadon, looking after Harry and Ferne.

Arthur Egbert, who gave blood with me and had no trouble.

184

The Scism family in 1940.

Isabel Hills, who led songs in Twin Falls for years, including 1938-40.

Oliver Brown, who used to sing in the Twin Falls Church before he was inducted into the Navy.

CHAPTER FIFTEEN

Twin Falls—The Evangelists and the Move

While we pastored in Twin Falls, we invited a number of evangelists to have meetings with us. I don't recall just the order in which they came or the year, but I do remember that Ruby Keyes was baptized in Jesus' name while we lived in the first rented parsonage in Twin Falls. She'd had quite a good ministry among the Assemblies of God, and up and down the coast people knew the Keyes family well. God blessed their ministry. One Assemblies of God member told me that part of the church they used at that time had been roped off because the congregation had dwindled so much. When the Keyes came, they had a real move of the Spirit, the revival lasted a long time, and the congregation built up. In the Keyes family, Sister Ruby was the main speaker.

Jane Moyer, my wife's youngest sister and Ruby's good friend, traveled with Ruby in meetings everywhere. Ruby's dad was a staunch Assemblies of God minister, but Ruby was willing to associate with us. She has said that the main thing convincing her to come to further truth was that I did not approach her in a rough or formidable manner regarding baptism in Jesus' name or the oneness of God in Christ. I did give her some literature when she and Jane came and asked her to read it when she had time because I felt it was well worth her taking time and effort to read. She later testified that, had I approached her in any other way, she might not have accepted this message.

After we had been there about a year and had moved into the second rented parsonage, Ruby Keyes and Jane Moyer came again. This time during their special services—they would sing together—I got wind that the congregation would vote on me. The First Pentecostal Church bylaws then ruled that if all the board members were satisfied with the pastor, the church would not need to vote annually, but that if one board member was dissatisfied, then the pastor's name would come before the congregation regarding retaining him or letting him go.

One night, the three members of the church board came to talk with me. Realizing the rather formidable situation, I had already written out my resignation, placing blame where I felt it belonged. After listening to what they had to say, I handed the resignation to them. I do not recall now their complaints, but they asked me to reconsider, which I did. They didn't vote and we stayed there, ultimately around five years.

When Ruby Keyes and Jane Moyer came on their second evangelistic trip, I had to travel back East somewhere. Since I was not taking the car and since the two ladies couldn't drive, I asked Arthur Hills, one of the young men in the church, to use it to take the ladies sightseeing around Twin Falls and wherever they needed to go. I came back, time went by, Arthur moved to Portland, and lo and behold!, I found out that this apparently had become the beginning of an interest between Jane Moyer and Arthur Hills.

On a still later visit by Ruby and Jane while we pastored in Twin Falls, we took them to Cascade for a revival, then started back the same day toward Twin Falls. The car slid on the ice and snow off the road and down toward the Payette River. We found security in a lodge. An old Swedish man there took us in very reluctantly. I had to search for help from the highway department, but the old Swede later warmed up to Marjorie and the children and Mother Moyer. Come to find out, this old man had been down to Ninth Street Mission and had been baptized there. Now he was back in the mountains and wanted to go back to Ninth Street Mission again to feel what he felt when he was there. Marjorie talked to him, explaining that he didn't have to go back to Oakland to feel God's Spirit. Later, the young people in our church in Twin collected money and sent a Bible to him. Years later, he passed away in a hospital in Boise. We never can tell how much good we can do along life's way.

Not too many months later a letter arrived from Jane wanting to know if I would come to Portland to unite her and Arthur in marriage. This surprised Howard West (whom Jane had told she would never marry a preacher), not to speak of me. Apparently she'd made some adjustment along the line.

In Portland at the Presbyterian church where the vows would be solemnized, the caretaker wanted me to wear the robe that his pastor wore while participating in services. I felt like David with Saul's armor, so after his much insistence, I declined and united Arthur and Jane Hills in marriage. I had fun teasing Arthur during his lifetime about how things took place while I was gone. Now he was my brother-in-law by marriage. Unfortunately, while we were in India, he passed away. Arthur was a very fine boy. I leaned on him and Charlie Yadon so much.

Ruby Keyes later married John Klemin, a young California minister. She still has a wonderful ministry, and God has blessed them both as they have labored together for the Lord in North America, Argentina, and England. We have through the years thought so very much of them, remembering all the time that it was my privilege to baptize her in the name of Jesus in the First Pentecostal Church in Twin Falls many years ago.

While we still lived in the first rented house in Twin, I invited Oscar and Ruth Vouga for special meetings. They had taken a church in Houston years before, but preachers move around. During these revival meetings, he and Ruth lived in our backyard in a little trailer house they'd brought. While there, he told me that he'd go straight to Tennessee from Twin Falls. I knew he'd have a problem because he planned to go back to a preacher who'd had a problem with the Tennessee District Board. I spoke to him about it, but he went anyway. As a result, the Tennessee board placed charges with headquarters against Brother Vouga.

One thing I've always admired about Brother Vouga: he subjected himself to the brethren and listened to their advice, even though it might not have been what he desired. He had not listened to my advice, but then I wasn't an official connected with Tennessee. His evangelistic ministry and Bible teaching were very good. We invited him more than once to speak for us.

While we lived at the second house, we invited Jerry Osborne to evangelize in Twin Falls. In planning for his coming, I told Marjorie that since we only had two bedrooms and since it was winter, we would give the second bedroom, which we used for the children, to him, and she could take Harry and Ferne into our bedroom. I would sleep on the screened-in veranda, which we ordinarily used during the summer months, though it was not very warm during an Idaho winter.

First, I had said that I would sleep with Brother Osborne, but that was before he came. I tried it the first night, but I was really worn out the next day because he snored so loudly. My problem was that I could determine when he would catch his breath and be supplied with air for another snore. So my apprehension was that he was at the point of dying. After that one night, I told Marj I would take the porch and asked her to bring plenty of covers. Of course, Brother Osborne knew why I was leaving.

We had good meetings with Brother Osborne. The Lord blessed and we had a great time. During his meetings there, he wondered if I would object if he led "Love Lifted Me." He said that back in Texas they'd finish the whole song by the time we sang the first verse and chorus. I told him fine and made arrangements with our songleader of the evening, Isabel. He led the song and really finished it off in a hurry—full speed ahead.

During the time he was with us, the Seventh-day Adventists held special services in a Quonset hut that had sawdust shavings for a floor. We had no Saturday night or

191

Monday night service, and Brother Osborne wanted to visit the Seventh-day Adventists, so I drove him there one night, took Marj somewhere, and then rejoined him.

The Seventh-day people commented in their public addresses relative to various denominations, churches, and people. As we came out the doors together on our way out, Brother Osborne said that when they had taken up the offering, they'd said that if anyone had any question bothering them to write it down and drop it into the offering plate. Brother Osborne wanted to know their attitude concerning the Holy Ghost, so he put in that question. They had said that they would mail out literature on whatever topic or question had been asked. I told Brother Osborne, "You'll have a visitor." He said, "Oh, no, they'll just mail some literature on this—that'll take care of it all." I again affirmed to him that I felt he would definitely have a visitor.

One day very soon after, while I stood by the front door with a glass in hand looking out toward the street, I saw a Seventh-day Adventist elder driving by, looking at the numbers on the houses. When he looked at our house, he stopped his car, crossed the street, and came up to the door. I told Brother Osborne sitting in the living room, "He's here." The elder knocked on the door and wanted to know if a Jerry Osborne was there. I told him yes and cordially invited him to come into the house.

They settled down to have a little talk. In the midst of their conversation, this local elder of the Seventh-day church asked him if he had received the article on the question bothering him. Brother Osborne assured him that he had. The elder asked him what he thought about it. Brother Osborne really surprised me by saying, "I

192

thought it was very good for a man writing on a subject he knew nothing about. The only person qualified to write on that subject is one with the experience."

The poor local elder was quite flustered and embarrassed, and I could see his color rise above his collarbone and around his neck and face. They continued discussing until finally the elder invited Brother Osborne to attend Elder Kegley's lecture on that same subject the following Saturday night. He and I went and had an interesting experience, which led to nothing. They kept their same old position, and we kept ours.

I met Jerry Osborne again in 1944, while I was district superintendent of the Pentecostal Church, Incorporated, and on my way to the Jonesboro PCI Conference. I spent the night in Kansas City, ready to leave for Jonesboro on the Florida special. As I walked into the railway station, I saw a seated man wearing a homburg hat, and though his back was turned toward me, he certainly reminded me of Jerry Osborne. Sure enough, it was he, so we had a chance to visit before the train's departure time came. Brother Osborne wanted to know how I was traveling. I told him, coach. He wanted to know if we could sit together and I said, "Sure."

As we boarded the train, soldiers and their wives and friends greeted each other. Everyone was talking and the weather was hot. Brother Osborne sat by the window and I in the aisle seat. After things quieted down, I saw his head leaning forward. Suddenly, he emitted a very loud snore, awakening people sitting in that area. They began to giggle and laugh. Brother Osborne turned toward me and asked, "Did I snore?" I told him, "Brother Osborne, you sure did." At any rate, he'd sure not forgotten how to.

193

Before we arrived in Jonesboro, he wanted to know if I would be willing to share a room with him because it would save us both money. I agreed, providing that he have a separate bed to sleep in and that Brother Goss did not want the general board members housed together for convenience' sake—for example, if something came up and Brother Goss wanted the board to meet, they could do so more easily in what we now term the headquarters hotel. If this setup did not prevail, I'd be delighted to share a room with him. Since we'd stayed awake all night on the train, after we arrived in Jonesboro, we checked in the hotel where we planned to stay.

However, Brother Goss did want the board to stay together, so I had to vacate and move to the board's rooms. In our room, Dale Strubel and J. A. Johnson shared one double bed, while A. T. Morgan and I shared the other.

Since this was the last conference before the merger, naturally the merger came up as part of the discussion. Resolutions were passed before the actual merger did take place at Kiel Auditorium in St. Louis the following year.

That journey enlightened me in reference to Brother Osborne's continued ability to really snore. Before he left to return to Austin, Texas, he told me that if he knew he were going to die and had only one meal left, he would like above anything and everything else gravy and rice. Out West, we used potatoes and gravy, and only ate rice in deserts, but when we went in India, we learned to eat rice as a main diet.

I appreciated Brother Osborne's ministry very much. At one conference, he was asked, during the voting session between casting of ballots while the tabulating committee counted them, to tell his experiences. He would start, the committee would bring back a report, we'd vote on something else, and then Brother Osborne would pick his story right up from where he had stopped and carry on with it. This great man had our brethren's respect throughout our fellowship for many years.

While living in the same house in Twin Falls, we had another evangelist, Frank Slater, who originally came from England, then to Canada, then down into the States. He prayed more than any evangelist we had with us during those days—long, long hours in prayer. He also favored victory marches and had a lot of them in the Twin Falls church.

Being an independent person, he wanted to arrange things his way. For example, one day either Marjorie or her mother slipped into his bedroom while he was having breakfast and made up his bed. He went back, saw his bed all made up, and commented that he didn't want any "pesky women fooling around" in his room.

One time I had to go away. A. O. Moore had to go on a trip and Sister Moore was not well, so they asked me to speak in Rupert. I went on a Sunday and spoke there while Brother Slater was in Twin.

I noticed that during Brother Slater's preaching, his neck would swell and he'd loosen his tie and shirt collar. The veins on his neck would protrude and he'd really preach his heart out. I wondered many times if something might happen later on, and it did—ultimately, he had a nervous breakdown.

While he stayed with us, after one particularly good meeting one evening, we ate ice cream. We did not have it often because we didn't have the wherewithal to make ice cream possible frequently. Ferne was just a little girl.

Brother Slater diverted Ferne's attention to somewhere else, then reached over, took her ice cream, and ate it. Ferne has remembered that down through the years. He liked the children and had a lot of fun teasing them.

During those days we had gasoline rationing. We gave him some of our gas so that he could get from Twin Falls to Rupert for revival meetings there. He wrote a postcard back.

Another evangelist who came was Art Smith. He and his wife came from California. He would preach and they would sing duets. He'd play his guitar and sing solos. Among his many favorites was "Daughters of Jerusalem." We had a good meeting with them.

Later, I met them on furlough in 1955-56 in California. While there, we visited a church in Loomis and met one of the saints who had been with him in North Sacramento. I mentioned that we were scheduled to be with Brother Smith the following morning. This person seemed to question that because A. A. Allen was to be there in a meeting. I concluded that I should call Brother Smith long distance and find out whether we should come or not. He assured me that he had planned on this, so we arrived on Easter Sunday morning, but I found that they'd made no preparation to show slides by darkening the windows. We went ahead and showed them anyway.

During that Sunday morning service, one of the men stood up and motioned for the children to come. Come to find out, they had planned an Easter egg hunt, so the youngsters took off to engage in this, which disrupted our missionary service.

We had no church to go to that night, and since Brother Smith was involved in a cooperative effort regarding A. A.

Allen, we went to his meeting. Brother Smith was the only one of our Jesus Name faith on the platform, so he looked like a square peg in a round hole. I assume that this period of time was the beginning of Brother Smith's departure from the United Pentecostal Church.

Richard and Grace Goodenough visited us in Twin Falls during one summer for revival services. Sister Goodenough used to be Grace Pharr. She felt that she had a missionary call to China. They planned to go to the mission field. In the meantime, they became involved in evangelism in the United States. He preached well, and we had good services with them.

By 1943, we had been feeling for a while that we needed to make a change but didn't know where to go. I traveled by train all the way to Toronto, thinking that maybe that would be the Lord's will. (We didn't think about Chicago, in spite of that lady's "prophecy.") I visited the church now pastored by Carl Stephenson and stayed in the home of Brother and Sister Lynden, fine people in the church who, after every service, would have something to eat with a bit of tea. I'd talk with them, then look over to find my tea cup filled up again. Prior to this, I'd never been accustomed to drinking tea, but thus I acquired a taste for tea, useful in India. Brother Goss, the general superintendent of the PCI, who had lived in Toronto years ago when he was a member of the Assemblies of God, made these arrangements, and since he could not be there to introduce me, arranged for someone else to do this. This was my first introduction to eastern Canada. The church was very good to me, and the people very friendly.

The services were good, but I noticed that the people sat in separate groups, which made me wonder if sometime later the church would split. I told them I would let them know my decision. I prayed about it, and because I felt that someday the church would split and I did not want that to happen in my ministry, I declined. (Years later on furlough from India and with the pastor in Toronto, we found out that the church had split under his pastorate.)

Just before I left Toronto, the Lyndens' little girl seemed to be having trouble with mumps. I told the mother not to worry—our children had their problems, too, and came out of them. I began my journey west by train, arriving back in Twin Falls.

While we held revival meetings with Sister Lyerla shortly thereafter, I came down with mumps. This affected me very much.

Sister Lyerla was a midget and had to have her own pulpit. (Nowadays the thing that's short is our revivals—three days. If the people don't get revived in three days, forget it.)

While the revival was going on, she concluded that she had best move on somewhere else since she was staying at our house and I was coming down with mumps. I took her to the train station.

The church bought property for a parsonage across the street from the church building. I was there long enough to scrape it and paint it—it was in terrible shape.

While we lived there, Jet Stallones evangelized with us. She and her husband had briefly pastored me years ago in Salem, but he had since passed away. After the meetings with us, we were going to take her to Rupert for her meetings there. In the meantime, W. T. Witherspoon telephoned us from anniversary services with B. M. David at Bethel Temple, also in Twin. Brother Witherspoon's wife had passed away, so he was an eligible widower and had taken a strong liking to Sister Stallones. He wanted to take her to Rupert, but he had no car. These were the days of gas rationing, but we had offered to take her to Rupert, so when Brother Witherspoon needed a car, we offered ours.

Then Pastor B. M. David offered his. Almost at the last minute, Brother David said that "because of the problem between the two churches," Brother Witherspoon and Sister Stallones should not go to Rupert by themselves, but should have a chaperone. (He did not explain what Brother Witherspoon and Sister Stallones had to do with the fact that people unhappy with B. M. David had left Bethel Temple for years and had started the church I was now pastoring.) Only God knows what B. M. David had in mind when he said that PAJC Superintendent Witherspoon and Evangelist and Bible Teacher Stallones needed a chaperone. Brother Witherspoon and Sister Stallones were old enough to behave themselves.

Brother David called wanting to know if Marj and I would go as chaperones. Brother Witherspoon borrowed Brother David's car and came to pick up Sister Stallones. Sister Stallones had a big fortnighter suitcase that we would have to put in the trunk, but Brother David's car had a strange bumper guard that we had to lower before we could open the trunk. Brother Witherspoon and I finally figured out how it worked and got the fortnighter in. During the struggle while we tried to get the thing to work, Brother Witherspoon said, "It must be Persian." Brother David was.

Marjorie put on a nice dress, I adorned myself, as best as I was able, and we sat in the back seat of the car while Brother Witherspoon drove and Sister Stallones sat beside him. We carefully surveyed the scenery before us and had the privilege of escorting Brother Witherspoon and Sister Stallones as thus we wended our way from Twin Falls to Rupert. Then Brother Witherspoon drove us back to Twin Falls and went on his way.

I've often wondered what B. M. David was thinking in demanding a chaperone for Brother Witherspoon. I think probably he wanted to go himself, but Brother Witherspoon was just a little too quick for him and outsmarted the old fox.

Years later, after I became an honorary member of the UPC General Board, I told this story to the General Board, omitting the part about Brother Witherspoon calling the bumper guard Persian, considering it somehow irrelevant in the presence of Brother Nathaniel Urshan, the general superintendent, who is of Persian descent.

Ultimately, we were asked to pastor the church in Rupert. We immediately felt that it was the right thing to do, so we accepted.

Richard and Grace Goodenough, evangelists.

Frank Slater and his ice cream victim, Ferne.

Ellis and Marjoie Scism, Jet and W. T. Witherspoon. Apparently, the chaperoning worked.

Ruby Keyes, who joined the Scisms for revivals in 1938.

CHAPTER SIXTEEN

Rupert

*O*ne older member of the church, James Hruza, and his younger son, Melvin, brought a quarter of beef to the parsonage. That greatly helped us. James Hruza was a very faithful member of the church for many years.

I did carpentry work with Milba, Melvin's older brother, at the church. He worked as an accountant for a Ford dealer, and Milba's wife, Verna, taught school. Her sister, Bertha, was a county school superintendent. Milba and Verna's two children, Ronald and Audrene, formed close friendships with our children. Though Ronald and Harry once fought in a strawberry patch and Harry, who got the worst of it, came back covered with strawberry stains, they continued as very good friends to this day. When we had to leave Rupert, Harry felt he had lost his best friend and became very distraught. Just as we crossed the Idaho-Oregon state boundary, the heavens opened and started raining. I commented to Harry, "Oregon is weeping over the conditions in Idaho." Unfortunately, Harry did not agree with his father's idea, did not appreciate the joke, and still retained a very somber countenance.

Ferne would play with Audrene, too, very often. All four of the children played together. One day, Audrene, when she was eight or nine came to Marjorie and said, "Someday I'm going to marry Harry." Of course, at that time we had no idea this would really take place. They were child sweethearts who, years later after long separation, married after a year of Bible college.

Once in Rupert, Harry performed some misdemeanor that resulted in my announcement to him that he would receive a spanking. He arrived, unbeknown to me, with his back trouser pockets filled with wallets and, while the spanking progressed, emitted some very convincing cries. I would never have caught on except that, as he left the room, Ferne smiled at him. When I saw that smile, I knew something was afoot and later soon discovered the source. The second time, the hollering was in earnest.

Jay and Rose Craven faithfully attended the Rupert church, as they still do to this day, though Jay spent a lot of time in the army back then. I missed him very much while he worked in the service. Rose and her mother and sister would sing trios in church very often. They, too, attended very faithfully.

Wiley Craven, brother of Jay, and his wife, attended faithfully, as did Sister Craven's relatives, Brother and Sister Switzer.

Winton Walker, mother of Dale, faithfully taught Sunday school in the Rupert church for many years. For example, she taught Audrene and the other children not to use "golly," "gosh," "darn," or "gee," since they are just euphemisms for swearing—"God," "damn," and "Jesus." I'd met the Walkers in 1933, become friends in 1934, and was now their pastor. Dale was a strong young man in the church now.

Sister Gibson, also a member of the church, and her daughter Sister Palmeroy, though that wasn't her name then, attended. Sister Manning of Fenton, Missouri, is the third generation—a daughter of Sister Palmeroy.

Then there were Victor and Alvin Meier and Ethel, Alvin's wife. We were close to them. Later I dedicated a very lovely chapel that Victor built in Nampa, Idaho, for the glory of God and the good of souls. A catastrophe happened in the family when Alvin's son-in-law killed him. We don't always know why certain things happen, but they do even though we don't at the moment understand God's plan or purpose in it. They take place irrespective of our thinking. Later, the Meiers went into the Latter Rain Movement, but they still kept a soft spot in their hearts for us.

Some good evangelists visited us in Rupert. Wilbur C. preached in Rupert and the Lord blessed. One night he preached and came down on women's short hair, beauty parlors, and so on. Well, one faithful member of the church had a beauty parlor and a visitor was with her. The beauty parlor owner had been true to the Lord in the midst of a very great problem she'd had. Her husband, the deputy sheriff of Minidoka County, had tried to injure her. He'd also left her. The beauty parlor provided her only source of income, her only livelihood. This work she knew and had been doing for many years.

I wondered at the time, If he comes down this strongly,

how will she react? But in his offering that evening, she gave him a check for ten dollars—a lot in those days— so I thought, Well, she had ample grace to help her weather her situation again and again. I had great admiration for her.

Also while we pastored in Rupert, Nona Freeman and Gracie Yadon (a sister of Emmett, Haskell, Paul, Charlie, and Frank) came by and held missionary services for us.

Another evangelist who came was Ralph Glasgow. We traveled from Rupert, which has a much higher elevation, down to the lower Boise Valley. He wanted Ferne, who was just a little girl, to play the piano while he sang. He said he would sing a quartet, and we wondered how he would do this. He did it by taking all four parts and switching rapidly from one to another—quite humorous and very informative.

One Sunday morning, he came down hard in his sermon, warning the saints against talebearing. Previous to the service, he had told me one official had preached against tale bearing using a certain verse of Scripture but had engaged in talebearing at another time. Now Brother Ralph was taking the same verse of Scripture, so I wondered just where he would go with the sermon. When he was finished, he told the people he did not want them standing around doing a lot of talking, talebearing, gossiping, and finding fault, but to go right out the doors and straight home. One brother from Albion later told me that he had never gotten his wife out of church so quickly as he did the Sunday morning after Brother Glasgow preached that way. Of course, the Rupert church, as far as I knew, never had a lot of this type of thing going on anyway, but maybe that sermon helped keep it from deteriorating.

Of course, Brother Glasgow's ministry was not confined to that one Sunday morning message. The Lord blessed the services. One time he spoke very strongly about so many preachers exercising psychology rather than faith. He said they placed preeminence on psychology and asked the congregation how many believed that if he did pray, God would answer. A number of hands went up, so he started to pray a prayer having to do with food and asked that the Lord would supply extra money for us because he was staying with us. This extra money was to help feed him. He felt that we should have about ten dollars extra per week to see that he had plenty of food to eat, though he didn't put it quite like that.

Then Brother Glasgow laid the Bible out on the stand in front of the pulpit and asked the people to come up and put in what they had. Those were difficult days for everybody, but Old Grandpa James Hruza gave him a check that night for the amount he'd asked the Lord for.

After the service, Brother Glasgow (we were good friends) told me, "Brother Scism, I knew you were going down to the Lower Valley tomorrow." I was superintendent by that time and needed to go there for church business. So the money wasn't just for his food.

Still, he had a very good appetite. Marjorie always carefully had something on the table, not only at regular mealtime but after service as well. One evening, she had ice cream and cake. Brother Glasgow, who loved to sit and talk, would stay up until the wee hours of the morning if you felt you could physically stand it, which I did not. Still, for a while, we would talk. This particular evening after talking a while he told Marjorie that he wondered if she had anything substantial to eat, that his stomach had

207

"swallered up that ice cream and cake like a blotter does ink." Although Marjorie had to get to bed to get the children off to school the next day, she prepared substantial food for him and then went to bed. He and I had the food together.

Many years before, Brother Glasgow had gone to Abilene, Kansas, for special revival meetings with John Mark Opperman. They were both having a difficult time financially, so Brother Glasgow asked if Brother Opperman would object if they took a special offering and divided it between them. Brother Opperman favored the idea, so they took up the offering and raised about seventy-five dollars.

One sister in the church, very curious as to what this money would be used for, had very often testified about not telling God's secrets. If the Lord showed you something, you should keep it to yourself and not go around telling others that God had showed you this or that— "Keep it as a secret of the Lord." Brother Glasgow remembered this and told her, "Sister, that's a secret of the Lord." He said later that he heard no more from her concerning not telling God's secrets. However, this not telling people what he and Brother Opperman had done reacted unfavorably on Brother Glasgow, since he'd had the idea to begin with, and he was never invited back. The lesson is that one should be straightforward and let people know the purpose of offerings or special funds.

I invited him again. I saw him again at the 1944 PCI conference in Jonesboro, Arkansas. Many years later while I pastored in Tennessee, he would come by and preach for me many times. Time has gone by, and Brother Glasgow has since passed away. It will be good to see him again.

In 1944 we held the district conference in McCall, Idaho, where Vern Abbott pastored. I was elected district superintendent of the Northwestern District of the PCI. A. D. Hurt had been superintendent in 1936, J. A. Johnson in 1937-39, C. H. Yadon in 1940-42, Emmanuel Rohn in 1943, and I started in 1944.

At the same conference, the conference decided that its superintendent should go on the field full time. The Northwestern District in the PCI, and also at first in the United Pentecostal Church (UPC) consisted of Idaho, Oregon, Washington, Montana, Wyoming, British Columbia, and Alaska.

I was faced with a decision—choose to be pastor of the Rupert church or accept the responsibility of being full-time district superintendent. We ultimately chose to leave Rupert. It was hard to leave the church, but we felt this move was God's will.

The church wasn't happy. Wiley Craven blamed Brother Goss for putting me on the field full time. Dale Walker was there with his leg in a cast. He was so put out by my becoming a full-time superintendent that he hit his cast with a cane, and both of them were quite verbal in his expressions. Brother Goss had encouraged the move, but the vote of the ministers had brought it about.

The district gave me the option of living where I wanted to. We eventually moved to the Portland area, making Oregon City our home with Mother Moyer due to its more central location relative to rail and bus connections. In those days, the clergy received fare reductions on these modes of transport. (S. G. Norris once sent me a pass from Portland to Billings, Montana.)

Before I left Rupert, several other things happened. I

had advised Edwin Judd, who'd been drafted, to take non-combat service—offer to work in hospitals or whatever, as long as he did not have to bear arms. This he did and wrote me from the Lapine, Oregon, camp for conscientious objectors on July 25, 1944. After he entered the service, he served in India, visited Mother McCarty's old station, and did everything he could to help God's work in Bharosa Ghar, Bhatpar, Uttar Pradesh, North India.

I attended the 1944 PCI conference in Jonesboro, Arkansas. One black man wearing an armband that read, "Righteousness unto the Lord," came to the building of the congregation pastored by T. Richard Reed. They gave him a place to sit—exceptional for a black in Arkansas society back then. While B. H. Hite was bringing out a very beautiful message about the necessity of the Holy Ghost, this brother would keep speaking up and commenting loudly. This bothered Brother Hite, so finally he said to the congregation, "The right kind of noise is all right, and the wrong kind is all wrong, isn't it?" He made his mistake by not just making a declarative statement. When he added, "Isn't it?" the black man picked it up just as quick as could be and said, "Right you are, Doctor." That really caused a bit of mirth in the congregation, naturally at Brother Hite's expense.

But that was a good conference. The content, intent, and purpose were all justified in the subsequent conference when the PCI and PA of JC united under the name of the United Pentecostal Church.

Meanwhile, the Peterses had come from Louisiana to the Northwestern District and wanted to start a church in Green River, Wyoming, so the district helped them get located and settled. It was tough going—Green River was a railroad town lying down between the hills. Trains from California and from the Pacific Northwest would hook up in Green River and begin the journey east, changing at Cheyenne to engines with very high wheels, and make good time crossing the plains to our board meetings in St. Louis or wherever. Now, the train traffic is mainly freight.

Brother and Sister Peters really struggled, living in Green River's cold climate in a damp, cold, miserable basement. They also had organizational difficulties because they had already applied for ministerial license in Louisiana. E. L. Freeman had signed their application because they came from his church. The Northwest brethren appreciated their consecration and willingness to endure hardship because we all knew about facing difficulties wherever we were, but the Peterses' problems were unusual and still they carried on. They had particularly good jail meetings, which really helped to hold them there. They also wanted to build a building, and the government made some buildings available. We cautioned the Peters to make sure their title was clear. Meanwhile, Brother Freeman worked on their papers.

We sent them some funds, and when they did not need all the money, they returned it. We sent it back, anyway—twenty-five dollars per month to help them get things going.

Meanwhile, Neva Russell, who had been a member of our church, started a church in Jerome, Idaho. She wanted to give land for the building and asked for only 150 dollars, adding that if the district board did not feel to help her with it, she would trust the Lord, who would provide it from some other source. We on the district board felt it was only honorable to give a gift since she

211

was willing to deed the property completely over to the district, so we appealed to the district for this money and they responded.

One brother, who did not always adhere to what he read in the manual or to rules the district board passed, complained. I wrote to him September 26, "I gather that you did not read the letter too closely," and reminded him that when he was in Aberdeen, Washington, in a difficult situation, he had made an appeal himself, so that I felt he was obligated to those who had rescued him them.

Sister Russell's sister, Victory Walker, received a local license, then moved to her parents' home in Puyallup. Sister Russell wrote to me about her interest in working with Wycliffe Bible translators, which is done on a free basis, but she couldn't afford to.

She also retained her interest in missionary work, corresponding with Brother Stairs, Brother Vouga (who told her that the Belgian Congo was closed and suggested she start another church in the United States), Brother and Sister Sheets (missionaries in China), Kathryn Hendricks (also China), A. O. Moore (India), Sister Reganhardt (Liberia), and the Freemans (Africa).

Sister Russell studied in the school of linguistics at Briarcrest, Saskatchewan, where they taught her to rough it. They also taught her medicine, anthropology, and morphology. We sent her a gift to help her along. She also wrote of Sister Steiglitz and of Dr. Cameron Townsend, whom everyone called Uncle Cam. I don't know why she never went overseas—possibly the fare.

That December, World War II was definitely moving toward a conclusion, but Brother Howard West's selective service number came up. Since he was pastoring, he asked

212

me to write a letter to the Selective Board. I did and they fortunately changed his classification to 4D, which relieved him and enabled him to continue his pastorate in New Westminster for a total of about twelve years. Within a month he was planning evangelistic meetings with Don Austin and Ralph Glasgow and missionary meetings with the Freemans. He still needed permission to live in Canada (he was from Caldwell, Idaho), so I wrote the draft board again, and they consented.

In early 1945, I traveled to Alaska. The main reason for the trip was that Sister Rose B. had gone to Sitka to open an orphanage with Brother and Sister French, who had already been there for years. She had a strong personality and things had not worked out well—Brother French and the mayor of Sitka had a problem involving her.

I had also received a letter from Sister Alice in Haines, Alaska. She reported having received her credentials and expressed gratitude for good meetings with Charlie Yadon, but added that Bill, her husband, had heart trouble and had become weary of his work and that they had trouble finding a place of worship. She requested that Walmer and Juanita Krausch come up and help them in the church, which was largely made up of children. She also mentioned that an Indian woman named Nellie was living with them and indicated that there was a problem with Nellie and Bill.

I took a train from Portland to Seattle. At the train station, this sister and one other met me. I asked them that if they had any charge against the husband to put something definite in writing, because unless I had something in writing, I could not take action. This they did not want to do, so I could only watch while up there in Alaska.

I then took a ship named the *Princess Louise* to Vancouver, British Columbia, and on a Sunday there had a couple of hours' layover, so I walked up the dock to see Brother Currie.

Back then, Brother Currie did not belong to the United Pentecostal Church, but to the Apostolic Church of Canada, though he strongly leaned toward our faith. He had strong convictions and was a sound, solid, good preacher of the gospel. He was also full of fun and would tell a lot of jokes. We all loved him very much. His first wife passed away and later on he married Sister Esther, who used to work with Helen Belden years ago—they had held meetings in Salem that I could remember. After Sister Esther became Sister Currie, she and her husband went out to Africa together.

On this day, church was about to start. Brother Currie walked back to the boat with me. He told me that just before leaving the church, he'd handed the service over to a sister and told her, "Now don't forget the offering," an admonishment with which every pastor will identify. After this congenial soul bid me goodbye at the dock, he left, and I sailed toward Juneau on the *Princess Louise*.

Army people sprinkled the ship. I shared a room with a colonel who was a doctor. The ship had posted the time of departure, and when the time came, they pulled the gangplank in. Very shortly afterward, a jeep roared up to me. An officer accompanied by an army nurse wanted the ship to stop, but they were informed that the ship could not stop. After a while we saw a boat come alongside the ship. They opened up one of the big doors down below. The nurse was furious because they would not help her get from the speedboat onto the ship. Ultimately she came up

214

on deck and talked to the doctor, complaining to him about them not giving her a hand. I know neither what he said to her or how she was mollified, but thought the incident amusing.

We went on to Juneau and found a place to stay for a few nights with some missionaries, one of them blind.

Then I traveled to Haines, Alaska, where I did not notice any particular incriminating item, just an excessive friendliness on the part of Bill and Nellie. Later on, things turned far to the worse.

Some of the saints were going several miles from Haines to Kulkwan for the smelt run. The mountain road had washed out, and we had to climb many little hills to get to the village. (Now they have a highway through there.)

At Klukwan, I had a very long conversation with Sister Norma, who was contemplating marrying Carl Omdahl, knowing that he had been previously married and wondering what I thought. He had in the meantime written me a statement of his divorce from his previous wife, who had been guilty of adultery, giving him grounds for remarrying. However, knowing the thinking of some of our brethren, I advised her to bear in mind that if she did marry him, some people would not accept her.

As things worked out, she did marry him and bore me no ill will for being honest with her in advice I felt would be most beneficial to her in days to come. She's been faithful for many years. Carl made a trip down south as an airplane pilot; his plane crashed into some electric wires and he died. She sent funds out to us in India to build a church in Carl's memory in the state of Kerala, which we did. She's been very good, thoughtful, kind, and helpful to us

215

through the years, and we have deeply appreciated her friendship all this time.

To go from Haines to Juneau I had to travel through Skagway at the foot of the mountains where the gold miners had gone long years ago during the Klondike Gold Rush. Skagway was very rough in 1945. On my way up, I hitched a ride on an army tugboat. The captain asked me to steer the tugboat while he went to have chow. He said, "All you have to do is stay within the orange markers. That's all there is to it." I told him I could handle that and at least did better than the *Exxon Valdez*.

We arrived in Skagway and I spent the night there. The next day, I caught a ride on a boat with twin Chrysler motors. We saw a lot of porpoise along that journey to Juneau, where I again stayed with the missionaries.

The next day, I began the trip to Sitka on a four-passenger pontoon plane. The pilot apparently had not piloted that particular plane on any previous occasion, because the man on the boardwalk beside the plane gave him flying lessons. After he got the motor running, we moved out into the bay. Then the motor died and another passenger, a rough old fellow from Mantesca Valley, pulled a silver dollar out of his pocket and said, "In God we trust. With everybody else, it's cash." "That joke may have originated then, but I doubt it's that new." Then we pulled out and up. I later learned that the reason the pilots flew over the landing area, then turned around and came back to land is so that they could make sure there was no log floating in the trough of any wave. If they would hit one, it would flip the plane.

By the time I got to Sitka, Sister Rose had already left and gone back to Boise, Idaho. I stayed with Brother and

Sister Kenneth French, went to see the mayor, and talked with him about the problem they'd had. Everything was resolved.

During that time at Sitka, I met Charlie Yadon, former teen from my pastorate in Twin Falls. He and I decided to go for a walk out from Sitka. While taking this walk, we saw bear tracks in the dirt. Then Charlie noticed that petals from a bush had not fallen into the bear track, leading us both to conclude that the better part of valor was to return to Sitka.

Later on, we both came back to the Lower Forty-Eight together. In St. Petersburg, Alaska, we visited Sister Norma's parents, and eventually sailed for Seattle on the _North Star_. While on the ship, Charlie sang and played gospel hymns on the piano. The people seemed to appreciate this very much; thus he became a witness no matter where he went. At Seattle we separated, and I traveled to Portland.

I called home along the way and talked to Marjorie, Harry, and Ferne. When I talked with Harry, he felt so bad that, hearing my voice and not having me there, he said it would have been better if I had not called at all. He was about eleven. After I came home, Marj told me his eyes had filled with tears as he said it.

I arrived in Bend, Oregon, and at the bus station tried to find out when I could get a bus from Bend to Twin the next day since I had a service with Harriet Marling, pastor in Bend, that night. I already had a ticket. I was told that no bus was available until the next afternoon, but a responsible-looking man in the bus station heard what I'd said and came up to tell me that he and another man were driving from Bend to Boise, leaving early the next morning. He offered a ride; I accepted. On the way from Bend to Boise, they paid for my meal. We went to a garage in Boise, where he had some repairs done to the car. While there, he invited me to ride on to Twin Falls since, he said, they were going to Twin Falls and I looked like a decent individual. (Of course, I looked a little better in those days.) After arriving at the bus station in Twin Falls, I thanked him profusely. Then he introduced himself as Mr. Hoover, the owner of Trailways. He told me he'd enjoyed the trip.

In April, a month or two later, the Allies overran Berlin and I moved to Oregon City.

Harry and Ferne

Ferne and Harry

219

Ellis Scism and Lyerla, midget evangelist, 1943.

CHAPTER SEVENTEEN

Starting Full Time

As previously explained, the 1944 Pentecostal Church, Incorporated, district conference in McCall, Idaho, voted to put the district superintendent on the field full time, so I had to decide whether I wanted to do this or remain pastoring the Rupert church. Though we had only pastored in Rupert about a year and a half, I did not feel that refraining from holding the office the district had asked me to perform would be pleasing to the Lord, so I chose to leave Rupert.

Perhaps it was a little unusual to create a full-time position when the organization would, technically, cease to exist after a year, but we took a step by faith, and it worked out for the next four years for us and for my successor, J. A. Johnson.

Harry had found a warm friend in Ronald Hruza and did not want to leave Rupert. Ferne had her school and church friends, too, but we knew they'd make friends in Oregon City.

In April 1945, while Hitler was meeting with some unpleasantness in Berlin, we had troubles of our own. Alvin Kantola, father of Donna, Darlene, and Gary, brought his truck from Cascade to Rupert. We loaded it up, and also a trailer we'd purchased from Sam McClain, which Howard Goss had given him at the conference in Houston during the time when Brother McClain had pastored in Rupert and I in Twin. Brother McClain had taken Brother Goss's daughters to Bible college in Boise. Brother McClain, Brother Goss's two daughters, Glen Walker, and I had all come back from the conference together.

While in Twin, I'd asked Brother McClain, "How about selling me that trailer?" and he'd sold it to me for thirteen dollars (yes, only thirteen dollars). We'd used it moving from Twin Falls to Rupert and now hooked it to Brother Alvin's truck. Following the truck were Marjorie, Harry, Ferne, and I in our car. Eugene McClintock, pastor in Jerome, drove the car part of the time while I rode in the truck.

The trailer gave us some excitement just west of Huntington, Oregon. Since it hadn't been bolted together properly (Brother McClain's improvements had not been substantial and neither had mine, since I didn't know how poorly it had been constructed—a few nails here and there, some long and some short) and the tongue was made of pipe, the trailer hitch broke. The safety chains kept the trailer behind the truck, but since we'd loaded the trailer heavily in front, the tongue dropped down on the pavement and sparks flew. Our problem was how to tell Brother Kantola, who wasn't aware of this. I slowly gained on the truck, drove the car alongside it, and gestured to him. He stopped. After we went back to Huntington in the car and bought parts, repairs were effected and we proceeded west.

By the time we got near Hood River, the load had bounced toward the back, so that when the bolt holding the trailer tongue to the trailer itself vibrated loose, the trailer tipped back and started jackknifing back and forth, left and right, cutting capers such that this time Brothers Kantola and McClintock knew something was definitely wrong. We stopped, tightened the nut, and reloaded the trailer. That was our last problem; we went on safely to Mother Moyer's place in Oregon City, where we unloaded. That same evening, Al and Brother McClintock started back. I certainly did appreciate Brother Kantola's great help to us by driving a long way in order to help us move from Rupert to Oregon City—we never could have made it without him. He was a true friend until he died of cancer many years later.

We moved to Oregon City, where Harry and Ferne started school. I bought some needed things to help furnish the home a little, and there was the matter of needing a portable typewriter. We bought a Remington Noiseless, which we eventually took to India. We also bought a Standard L. C. Smith, which I used extensively and also took to India in 1949, where I continued to use it even when this book's other author was a little boy.

In the meantime, since the PCI had no church in Oregon City, our family attended now and then (when we weren't traveling) at Andrew C. Baker's independent church, and Marj and the children went there while I traveled in the district. Brother Baker occasionally fellowshiped with the Pentecostal Assemblies of Jesus Christ (PAJC) and the Pentecostal Assemblies of the World

(PAW) and with independent ministers. He was quite senior at this time—a good evangelist and Bible teacher, a good singer and a very firm man. If he and B. M. David had freed more of their young men to evangelize outside their churches, I feel that the UPC would have more churches in the Northwest today.

Eventually, Brother Baker's church declined in attendance, Brother Baker died, and his son Oliver pastored there. Ultimately Edwin Judd, who attended that church for years and later taught Bible college at Pentecostal Bible Institute and Conquerors Bible College, started a church in Oregon City. It was pastored many years later by Gary Gleason, whose father I'd heard sing in the Gleason Quartet when I was a boy.

I attended the PCI's last general conference, mentioned already. None of us knew whether the merger resolution with the PAJC would pass or not, though we thought it would. A. T. Morgan and I shared a bed at that conference (his snoring wasn't as bad as Jerry Osborne's).

How does the work of a full-time district superintendent differ from a part-time superintendent's? Since I had no local church responsibilities, I visited churches in the district separated by few miles or five hundred miles. Since the district had no magazine, many pastors depended on me for news about what was going on in other churches. Finally, I had to counsel workers, encourage them, speak from time to time, dedicate church buildings, conduct business meetings that I would not otherwise be able to conduct, organize departments, and troubleshoot. This was very important for a small district, and we had an immense land area—Wyoming, Montana, Idaho, Oregon, Washington, British Columbia, and Alaska. Traveling itself took lots of time.

Brother Maulden, meanwhile, brought word to me from down east in Canada tipping me off as to what was in the wind: Wynn Stairs, head of Foreign Missions, planned to come out to our district. I would receive a letter from him saying that he would enjoy coming out to meet with the Northwest brethren again; his objective was to see the Wines, against whom someone had made an accusation.

When Brother Stairs came, the board met. We had made up our minds prior to his coming that unless he had some reason to cause us to change our thinking, we would still stand in support of the Wines and endorse their return to India. When Brother Stairs came, he could or would not supply us with the evidence we felt we would be justified in receiving. Brother Stairs commented that if he could not get the Northwestern District Board of the PCI to withdraw their endorsement of Brother and Sister Wine and family, then the missionary board would take that responsibility. That was what we thought they should do anyway, since they, not we, had the evidence. Not long after that, the Wines left our fellowship and branched into other work. The good Lord knows what situations worked out for them during their days with the Latter Rain Movement.

One night I had a telephone call from Sister Lowe in Montesano to come and bring anything and everything with me to help them prove their entity. The congregation there had a very large building where they met for service and where the pastor lived—a three-story building with a large basement. Three trustees elected by the people held this property, but they had no membership roll, so when they wanted to sell the property and in turn buy a regular church building, the real estate agent asked who they were and how they could prove their entity since they had no bylaws, no membership roll, nothing.

We met in Montesano, and a brother who had opposed organizing under the name of the PCI realized the advisability of making a definite change. As a result, they organized that night, established a membership roll, and in the due process of time could dispose of the old building and purchase the new, the dedication services of which I later attended.

The coming merger meant more churches to visit. Sometimes our district youth leader, Vernon Nepstad, and I spent happy times traveling from place to place in behalf of the Lord's work scattered here and there throughout the district. We corresponded heavily due to our travels.

He had trouble understanding what went on in district board meetings, so I suggested to the brethren that we let him sit in on board meetings to give him a little idea of what went on—our problems, our joys, etc. The brethren went along with the idea. He seemed to appreciate very much that act of kindness toward him. He married Ethel, a young girl whom I used to teach in Sunday school in Oakland, California, and he later pastored in Yakima. He took the church under difficult circumstances, including the ministry of a free-lance preacher who had tried to hold the services before Brother Nepstad took the church, and he had made some stipulations and requirements that he felt he needed in order to pastor the church. The people complied with them at first, but before long things didn't work out too well for him. He had plenty of problems with the church, particularly with one brother, and the district had a bit of a problem with him because Brother Vernon was inclined to make many requirements and question those in positions of leadership.

Once he had a problem with Ruby Keyes (now Klemin), purely from a lack of understanding on Vernon's part concerning the policy that the PCI worked under. So many times we find lack of understanding due to people not having read or making sure they comprehend exactly what the bylaws state.

Eventually, Vernon resigned the Yakima church. He wanted to start another in the city, but the members of the district board did not feel at liberty to permit him to start another work in opposition to the existing work. I took this position for the same reason that I had stood by our PCI pastor in Yakima years before when Brother Vouga had wanted to start a church in opposition to the British Israel teaching that the existing pastor possibly espoused. Although I do not believe in British Israelism, yet the existing church did belong to the organization and I felt it my duty to stand by our pastor. Of course, now the picture has changed: the United Pentecostal Church has its own church in Yakima, and the Lord has blessed.

Also in 1945, the PCI and PAJC held simultaneous conferences at Kiel Auditorium in St. Louis. The day meetings were separate, the night meetings together. Earlier, Brother Witherspoon, who was superintendent of the PAJC, had written a fundamental doctrine for a merged organization while visiting the PCI church pastored by Brother Branding. A minority in the PCI did not believe that water baptism or a tongues experience was essential to salvation. Brother Witherspoon's statement gave room for them until we would all come to a unity of the faith.

Now that we had merged nationally, each district would

227

have a merged conference. District lines were those set up by the PCI. We'd always had good fellowship with the PAJC and the PAW, but now, because we were merging with the PAJC, we had had our district conference together. Due to my wife's illness, I had to miss the board meetings and asked Brother Maulden, the western Washington presbyter, to sit in as my proxy with the rest of the board members of both boards—PAJC and PCI. This he did, and very well, too, though one of the brethren raised some question concerning him doing this on grounds that he was a turkey farmer (he kept some turkeys).

When I look back over the years, I look at those who have been instrumental, those who stood with me. Brother Maulden stood with me and with the board. He may not have agreed with every item, but that's only natural, each having his own opinion. Yet he willingly laid down his own particular opinions for the sake of overall harmony, and not all people did this—sometimes, indeed, quite the reverse.

Because the constituency had changed, we needed new elections. We held a merged district conference in Pendleton, Oregon, at the Christian Church. B. M. David was district superintendent for the PAJC, and I was for the PCI. He came down to our mission in Pendleton to talk with me. He said he would not give up his church to become the district superintendent because he had a good church, but that he would be the district assistant superintendent (there was no such office). I told him that we had nothing to do with what the conference might decide.

Brother Goss was the presiding chairman. Brother David and I sat on the platform. As they passed out the ballots, Brother David said to me, "We must give them some names to vote on." I again said that this was the nominating ballot and that whoever the people chose was their business. I was elected and continued my work.

I noticed no hesitation by former PAJC ministers to accept me as their district superintendent—other than B. M. David. I continued my district work in the enlarged district.

At Caldwell, years before, some member of Emmanuel Rohn's church had padlocked him out of his church building. He left that church and started another congregation in Caldwell, and the original church Robert Hammond, Sr., eventually pastored. Brother Hammond had been a member of the former PAJC, but since I was now superintendent of the merged fellowship, I had the responsibility and joy of visiting his church as well as the other.

Once at a church dedication meeting at the old theater building in Tacoma, I introduced Brother Currie to the brethren. Brother Currie had with him a Brother Deverill, whose name I made the mistake of not writing down on a piece of paper, which I normally would have done. In the introduction I wanted to introduce Brother Deverill (who later passed away in Africa), but I only got as far as "devil" and then didn't know where to go from there. Brother Currie rode me very, very heavy about that for a long, long time. Since Brothers C. H. Yadon, Currie, Deverill, and I all stayed together and would ride to and from the old theater where the church worship was, Brother Currie had a lot of fun teasing me.

He enjoyed telling many funny stories during meetings with Brother Benedict until Brother Benedict's boy in a testimony service said, "Who wouldn't receive the Holy Spirit with Brother Currie's ministry—he tells so many jokes." We all had a good laugh at that, but, seriously, Brother Currie was a very good minister. Unfortunately he was very strong on the doctrine of eternal security, but we had fellowship with him down through the years, because he was never contentious about it.

Margaret Shalm came out of Brother Currie's church. George Shalm first met her there.

We had many problems during those days. Sometimes pastors would stay at a church a short while and then change. For example, one brother resigned a church in McCleary, Washington, then in Pocatello, Idaho. Another brother came to Salem, Oregon, then left, then came back again.

Of course, sometimes the pastors had good reasons. Carl Adams resigned the church in Tacoma due to his poor health. The Sunday before I arrived, he started to resign, but just couldn't go ahead and carry it through. After I arrived, his father asked me to read the resignation letter.

Some willingly worked and sacrificed. Ernest Moyer, my wife's brother, took the pastorate in Kellogg Park in 1945. He would later start several churches in the Portland area, as well as an old folks' home and a Bible college. I've often wondered at the little recognition he has received for all he has done, but a day of reckoning will come when he will receive the reward for all he's done in the Portland area for God's kingdom.

In July, Stella Peterson lived in Walla Walla, Washington, strong on the message and yet needing fellowship. She mentioned the Crumpackers, who had gone back to the Methodist Church, as well as someone about whom I knew nothing. I wrote to her, "We are distinctly Oneness people," underlining "Oneness," and referred her to Brother Flatbush in Pendleton, at that time her nearest neighbor. She wanted to visit the Lewiston church for watchnight service.

In November, Arthur Egbert, who had donated blood with me, was working in McCall, Idaho. He'd received various opportunities to help works, all of them involving small places and requiring him to hold a job and work, but that often happens with our brethren. They had two feet of snow up there. The work at New Meadows had opened up and the church at Klamath Falls wanted a pastor.

By December, Sister Alice wrote to say that Brother Bill had refused to ask Nellie, the Indian lady living at their house, to leave. I had not been able to do anything about this because Alice had refused to place charges.

On January 2, 1946, I wrote to Bill wishing him a Merry Christmas. I gave family news, mentioning that my mother and father had visited us for Christmas, that we'd enjoyed this privilege of their visit for the first time in many years due to Mother's ill health, and that I felt especially grateful to the Lord that we could spend Christmas with them. (It would be our last Christmas together—Mother died that year.) I told him that Harry and Ferne looked forward with incomplete happiness and with the possibility of considerable reluctance to the idea of going back to school, but that they had no way out and that they'd soon swing into line and enjoy school.

I concluded with some advice for Bill, expressing my concern about his actions and his spiritual condition. I suggested that he come down to the States, not pressuring him, because that wasn't the idea. I knew he worked in a hardware store at that time and that the town had much tuberculosis. I tried to encourage him to come home to have fellowship with the brethren and get out of that atmosphere, which no doubt would have greatly helped him. I knew he was accumulating a home and all, but accumulation, if it grows more important than spirituality, becomes destructive. But he didn't come back, and eventually I refused to sign his license credentials because of what was going on. Later, Alice went back to Alaska against Bill's wishes, and both she and the other lady lived in the same house until ultimately Bill had to provide another place for Nellie to live.

Bill had pastored in Ellensburg, on the coast, and had involved himself in the Lord's work in more ways than one. He and his wife used to sing together and play the piano, and outwardly everything looked fine, but inside was one of those heart-rending situations that beset people from time to time and in which one wonders what to do and that does not end successfully, regardless of what one would hope. It tore up Alice because she knew that Bill did not love her as a husband should love his wife. Bill was very bitter against a lady in the Juneau church because she wrote about the situation. When Alice helped take care of the Juneau church, they sent Bill a bill of ninety dollars for her expenses to stir him up as to his family responsibilities—but Bill didn't see it like that.

Eventually he lived a double life—part of the time with Alice and the children, the other with Nellie. A man in charge of the Bureau of Indian Affairs wanted Alice to do something legal to get the matter under better control, but she still hung on to the hope that somehow, someday Bill would be restored to the Lord, but eventually Bill married Nellie. The situation broke my heart.

Grace Scism shortly before her death in 1946.

Grace Scism's funeral, 1946.

CHAPTER EIGHTEEN

Continuing Full Time

*B*y late 1945, I was trying to locate a slightly bigger car than the 1939 Chevy I'd purchased in Rupert. We had long drives between churches, and too often at the end I'd be very weary and feel the need of a little rest before going into service and speaking, so I needed a car more conducive to comfort.

While we looked for a used car, one man asked if a new Hudson would interest us. I told him of course, but to be interested and to be able to do something about it were altogether different situations. He went on to explain that quite possibly he could arrange for me to have a new car fitting my needs without an unduly discomfiting expense. We took a look at a 1946 Hudson lacking a back seat, but he said that he'd get that later.

The United Pentecostal Church district conference would come soon in Rupert, so we borrowed some money from a young lady friend of Marjorie's and bought the car. We used a temporary back seat until the regular seat came several months later. My brother-in-law, Ernest Moyer, traded in his Plymouth and bought my Chevy.

Then my father, my wife's parents, Marjorie, the children, and I all left Oregon, going across the Columbia River on the Washington side (before the interstates, the Washington side of the river had a much better highway) to the conference in Twin Falls.

While we traveled on our way, a deer jumped off the bluff right in front of my new car. I hit it, of course, hurt the deer, and damaged the new car's grill work. Some men driving behind us in a pickup had some tools with which they finished it off. (the deer, not the car). It was brutal, but to leave the deer to die slowly would be worse. Besides, we couldn't leave it there—we had to take it to the next town and report it to proper authorities, who would hand the animal over to a home there to feed the elderly. We went on our way.

The radiator had a little disturbance, but the car worked, and after we finished our time in Idaho and returned back to Portland, I had the grill work replaced and everything fixed. We continued using that car until we left for India—a very roomy, comfortable car that my long limbs appreciated more than words can express.

By March, Stella Peterson was having services in Kennewick. Since I had inquired about her ordination, she told me, "I was ordained by Brother Gall and Brother Underwood of Belleville, Illinois. I've been holding credentials since 1931."

By June, Sister Stella was enthused about Brother and Sister Sheets, former missionaries to China. Sister Sheets had formerly been Alice Kugler, gone to China as a single missionary, come into this truth while out there, returned to the States and married Brother Sheets.

Brother Emmanuel Rohn hadn't written to me for some time after the election in 1944, but he finally broke the silence with a telegram by asking me the dates of the sectional prayer conference so that he could set the dates for his church building dedication. Later we exchanged travel plans, and since Brother Rohn was starting a school, I sent him a book by Carl Smith, who was with the PAW, entitled *A Scriptural View of the Christian Pastor*, thinking it would benefit him.

In mid 1946, Mother Moyer sold her place in Oregon City and bought property in Portland. Her husband had served in the Spanish-American War, which gave her a small pension, but she was unable to make payments on a house. She paid for the new property with the price of her old house and by rental income from apartments within the new. We too paid rent while we lived there until we left for India. Today Rene Higgins, her granddaughter, and her husband, Joe, live there with their three beautiful children.

That same year, since Brother Norris from St. Paul was going to visit B. M. David in Twin Falls, and since we were now a merged organization, I encouraged Brother Sweeten to invite Brother Norris to be with him in Rupert. We needed to encourage the unity of the faith.

During 1946 I corresponded extensively with Cecil Soper, who used to fill in for Brother Morse during the latter's annual vacation in my early Oakland days. During the last two years he had ministered with Brothers Goss and Vouga in Houston, and he'd seen a new Bible college,

Pentecostal Bible Institute (PBI), founded in Tupelo, Mississippi. We sent many Northwestern students there since we did not have a Bible college in the Northwest at all. God blessed PBI, and now it is Jackson College of Ministries.

In 1946, Alvin Kantola sent in his application to study at PBI. Of course, he could only go during certain seasons of the year—only when he couldn't farm. Audrey Lawler did, too, as did Dale Walker.

When the question had come up as to whether or not the organization should purchase the Tupelo property, I had voted for it, but the brethren did not see it that way, so the general body did not purchase the property and PBI did not become a national school. Still, interest remained high and, by 1947, Eugene McClintock was applying to go to PBI. Then went Eleanor Wilson, Jewell Yadon, Berniece Davis, and many others.

Possibly in 1946 (after the merger, at any rate), I received a copy of a letter notifying all district superintendents that a trial of Ralph Bullock would come up in California and requesting us to attend. At this time Brother Bullock did missionary work in Kowloon, Hong Kong. I'd heard rumors before this that he'd had an affair, and because he was my old mentor, I decided to go. I did not believe that he was totally guilty of the accusations, and Sister Bullock asked me, before everyone went into the hotel conference room, to make sure he had a fair trial. The more I sat, listened, and weighed the matter, the more convinced I became that he had been involved with two women.

Our family had come to baptism in Jesus' name under Ralph Bullock's ministry (Andrew C. Baker had conducted the baptism long afterward). I was a protégé of his, and now I was supposed to sit in judgment—a rather hard role to fill, but we had to do the right thing.

After Ralph Bullock knew my decision, he wrote me personally expressing his deep regret that I had not stood by him. You can't receive a letter like that from your father in the gospel without it hurting. I would meet Ralph Bullock again in Hong Kong.

In 1946, my mother's health deteriorated further. One of her legs was amputated just below the knee due to diabetes, an illness that gave her untold difficulty. The doctors didn't have the medication for it then that they do now. She was never strong enough to walk on crutches, so she spent the rest of her life in a wheelchair. Mother and Dad decided to sell their land in Silverton and move to Salem, where they bought a little prune orchard of about a couple of acres. Then they decided that rather than live out there, they would move to an apartment on Ferry Street above the mission. They lived there when, just before the general conference, I contacted a doctor, who said I would have plenty of time to see her after the conference.

Meanwhile, one of our brethren offered to pay my airfare should I have to return in a hurry. I left Portland in my car with Ernest and Alleen Moyer, Mother Moyer, and Myrtle, a young lady from the Portland church pastored by Brother Moyer. We dropped off Mother Moyer in Pueblo on the way to St. Louis.

At the 1946 general conference, I believe, Brother Goss, the general superintendent, called the board together because of a confrontation between him and S. G. Norris, head of Apostolic Bible Institute in St. Paul, regarding the new birth.

At the conference, Brother Goss explained in part the difference between his view and that of Brother Norris. God moved in a very pronounced manner and anointed B. H. Hite, district superintendent of Missouri, in a very unusual way at the board meeting. He gave a very forceful talk to the brethren, explaining that he felt differences in usage of words had caused the disagreement. He felt that we all had the same thought and same mind, and that differences lay in method of explanation.

This remarkable address helped break down some of the hard edges of attitudes some brethren at the meeting had displayed. After Brother Hite's address, the brethren all held together and hugged each other. Differences broke down, and everyone had a very mellow spirit of fellowship. People threw their arms around each other, weeping and crying, melting down and loving each other. Brother Norris followed me out to the kitchen to get a drink of water, where he told me he couldn't "stand up to that old boy," meaning Brother Hite.

Later I wrote to Brother Norris a quite frank letter. I felt that it was a little too early after the unification of the two organizations to start quarreling and that he was unfairly targeting Brother Goss. I didn't feel I'd want my children influenced by this example while they attended Bible college. That was putting it rather strongly, but that's how I felt because of the issues he had raised and the timing of the resolution he had presented.

Of course, I had the utmost respect for S. G. Norris. He treated us very, very kindly through the years—I could never ask a man to be more considerate, loving, and concerned than he was to us. We have found him to be a man who loves God, and after my return to America when my health hasn't been the best, he personified kindness to me in every respect. Our early disagreements were of the head, not of the heart.

While I attended this conference, a telegram came from two ladies from the Salem church advising that Mother was seriously ill and that I should return.

Our board meetings were held then much later at night then they are now. Around 3:00 AM, I phoned from my hotel room to the brother who'd offered to pay, but he made no effort to finance the plane fare, only offered his sympathies. I went to my brother-in-law, Ernest Moyer, who told me his finances were getting low, so we would drive as far as Denver. He drove most of the way, since I was so tired from being up night after night. I was really very weary. He dropped me off at the airport, then drove my car off to pick up Mother Moyer in Pueblo. I flew over the Rockies from Denver.

In flying from Denver to Salt Lake City, the plane—propeller driven, of course—had to cap some high elevations, and as we went up, I became very lightheaded. I had been told that if I would place my head between my knees, I'd feel better. The businessman sitting next to me noticed my problem—by that time I was beginning to perspire, too—so he reported to the flight attendant, who came with smelling salts. A whiff of that brought me around, but I still felt very uncomfortable.

After we landed in Salt Lake City, the flight attendant advised the new crew that during the next flight I should be given oxygen. I did not need a tank, since we wouldn't be traveling as high as when crossing the Rockies anyway, so I declined.

One very elderly lady on crutches amused me in the

midst of it all because she went through the whole journey without any trouble and got out ahead of me. She had to have help with her crutches, whereas I, a comparatively young fellow, could get along on my own steam, but she had come through just great, whereas I had all kinds of trouble. You never can know what's going to happen when you get up in these things. Now it's altogether different—pressurized cabins and a great pleasure to fly.

On arriving at Portland's airport, I took a taxi to my house to find no one there. I concluded that Marjorie was in Salem and that the children were with Art and Jane Hills and Ruby Keyes. I left by bus for Salem, where I found out that Mother was not as bad off as the two ladies sending the telegram had felt. She was still at home, not at the hospital.

Later, however, she became very ill, so we took her to Deaconess Hospital. The first two nights, we stayed with her. The third night, we asked the nurse her opinion. She felt Mother's feet, said they were warmer than the previous night, told us there was no particular danger, and advised us to go home and get our sleep, since we'd be needed the next night. But early the next morning, a man called to tell us that Mother had passed away. I've always regretted that I wasn't there when she died.

I couldn't have handled the funeral—George Eads did. I had made up my mind that I would stoically not cry at the funeral, but I cried, and I missed her for a long time afterward.

In October, Stella Peterson turned the work in Walla Walla to Brother Huffman, since she wouldn't be able to build until spring. She offered condolences over my mother's death, which I appreciated, since it deeply affected me.

By the end of 1946, I was concerned because the district was moving ahead much too slowly. All the easy places had been taken long ago, and I advised Dale Walker that a minister who wants to make an impact must adjust to life's difficulties as they come and go.

Bend campground, the Northwestern District campground until 1956.

CHAPTER NINETEEN

Concluding Full Time

On January 8, 1947, I wrote to R. T. Megrew about a boat. Brother Megrew, one of our very strong men many years ago in the message and a member of our district board, pastored near Seattle in a place called Ballard.

Kenneth French in Alaska, whom I had visited two years before, had requested a boat, but I couldn't find one of the right nature in Portland. Brother Opsand figured in the story because he knew about open-sea boats, and Brother Megrew finally located one named the Madura. They ultimately bought it, and met Coast Guard inspections and everything else related to maritime rules. Some thirteen brethren, including Howard West, journeyed to Alaska in it and had quite a time. They were seasick on the very troubled waters, an experience they do not recall altogether too fondly, but they made it.

Brother Stairs was out for the district conference when

we finished raising the finances to pay for the boat. Brother Emerson, the captain who took it up to Alaska, has since passed on to his reward. The boat proved to be a great blessing—Brother French could visit from one island to another and hold services in various places.

In the meantime, Hershel and Ruth Redmond wrote to me. I had met them in Oakland many years before. She had been raised in China by her parents, the Birdstens, missionaries with another church who had come across the truth through Brother Ewart's literature. Ruth had returned and experienced trouble speaking English after so many years speaking Chinese. One time she tried to say "dignified" and became so confused in her endeavors that she said "dingified." She was a fine person, and she married a fine man who had with his mother been putting out "Ping An News," a missionary newsletter from Southern California.

Now they planned to return to China as missionaries, but since sailing was a very uncertain thing and no one knew when they could book passage, Brother Hershel wanted to know about the possibility of pastoring a church until they could get passage to sail. Brother Johnson showed Brother Redmond around different places and tried to help him get started.

In the meantime, he wrote to me wondering about Klamath Falls, Oregon, willing to accept whatever would open up for him where he might serve the Lord. He mentioned that Sister Steiglitz and Sister Kathryn Hendricks would be going to the same place until they could book passage. I don't know what happened in California, but Klamath Falls was not possible since they could only come with just their suitcases and we had no place for them to stay or financial aid to give. Whoever took the work would take responsibility not only for personal living but also the total responsibility of payments for the church. I suggested Billings, Montana; Eugene, Oregon; and a missionary group in Salem.

Then Sister Ruth passed away, and Hershel was heartbroken, but God had been and still was with him and brought him through.

In late January, I received information from George Glass, district secretary of Louisiana, that the application of the Peterses had come to him. Due to our financial limitations, the district couldn't do much for the Peterses, but we did send Bibles and New Testaments. Due to their financial limitations, they couldn't always come to conferences, but we did appreciate the times they made it. Eventually they bought some kind of railway building, then later a trailer, and today we have a nice church in Green River.

Later, Victoria Walker went to Green River. Berniece Davis was in Superior, several miles away. When you travel in those wide-open spaces you discover that the spaces are indeed wide open.

On February 13, 1947, I performed the wedding ceremony for Laverne Brown and Eugene McClintock, our pastor in Twin Falls. The wedding was held in the First Church. Frank Maulden participated. Brother McClintock loves to tell everyone that I accidentally sat on their wedding cake in his car. Some things I'd rather forget.

The next week, I dedicated the church building in Kennewick, Washington. When I met Brother and Sister Rohn at this meeting, Sister Rohn did not look at all well. I also visited Boise and had a missionary conference in Rupert.

247

Many events happened like this all through 1944-48.

In 1947, Brother Peter Shebley wrote me a long letter concerning William Branham. He had been with Brother Kidson and with Brother Branham back East in Arkansas. At Camden, Arkansas, a picture had been taken of Brother Branham with a halo over his head. This photo was publicized a great deal and made quite an impression for a time, but time too has a way of dealing with all things.

For a time it appeared as if Brother Branham was taking a very firm stand along with our brethren. Brother Kidson was his business manager then. Peter Shebley wanted me as district superintendent to invite William Branham to use Portland as a base for hub activity. Peter Shebley asked Ernest Moyer as district secretary the same thing. We didn't.

William Branham came to Portland anyway after his meeting in Vancouver, and Gordon Lindsay was his manager. Brother Kidson couldn't come. They had their meetings at Benson Polytechnic High School, and I wouldn't go on the platform that first meeting because of a publication two church groups had put out in which he stated his method of baptism. We made copies and circulated them in the district. We raised an issue concerning it, and I did not want to identify myself with the meeting. Being the leader in the district, I kept aloof from and stayed out until many of our brethren from the district would come to make it a truly joint meeting (which it had been advertised as, but which in reality was not carried through in the end). The Shebleys met Brother Branham, and he wrote out his baptismal formula, which our brethren could not accept.

Also in 1947, Brother Garrett, a protégé of W. E. Kidson

who had quite a healing ministry for some time until he eventually went to the Philippines, held meetings in Tacoma, then with Brother Kidson and with Brother Branham. They ended up in Fresno, California. Brother Branham requested that I come and paid my plane fare from Boise, Idaho, to Fresno, and then from Fresno back to Portland. He was considering becoming part of what he termed a "greater fellowship," trying to involve groups from different faiths—trinitarian brethren and whoever else would participate with him. I roomed with Gordon Lindsay, who asked me to call Jack Moore.

Afterward, I walked with Brother Kidson down to the bank and told him what I'd heard was going to happen. Brother Kidson didn't believe it. Then Brother Lindsay left the meeting and the town. Brothers Branham and Kidson were going to take the midnight train south and wanted to occupy the room Brother Lindsay and I had been in. Brother Kidson asked me not to go into the room until after they had left, so I sat around the vestibule.

The Armenian people sponsored the meeting. They thought very much of Brother Branham in those days—if he had been candy, they would have eaten him alive. As it was, they gave quite generously to help.

That night, Brother Kidson (whom Earl Toole, father of Winfred Toole, drove to and from the auditorium and hotel) forgot the offering and went back to the auditorium to get it. In the meantime, I decided that I wasn't going to just sit in the vestibule and wait and wait, but would go on up to my room, so I did.

That left me in the room with William Branham. We talked together and he affirmed his conviction. I wanted to hear this because of what he'd said in Portland about how

249

he was baptized—he had not taken a clear scriptural stand on his method. In our discussion, he raised his hand before the Lord and said he had not changed. I had known his doctrinal position before because his meetings had been with our brethren, but men do have the privilege of changing their doctrinal beliefs.

Later, but still in my superintendency, I was with him in a meeting in Oakland, where I'd taken some people down to be prayed for by him. There I observed certain things that I did not feel too happy about. By this time, my confidence in William Branham had pretty well been taken care of.

Too many men try to bridge the gulf between what we stand for and whatever other beliefs individuals may hold. This does not work out well. Time has proven that our position is biblical and correct and one worth standing for in spite of doubts, fears, and problems along the way.

On this journey, we came back up the coast through the redwood forest, which my dad had never seen in his life, and back into the harness of the work again. By 1948, Gordon Lindsay and Jack Moore were working out William Branham's schedule, but I was disenchanted with it and concentrated on my work in the Northwest.

About this time, Neva Russell, who'd been studying linguistics in Canada, asked if she could borrow money from the district in order to return to the school. Brother Hurt had offered to pay her tuition if she would agree to teach in his Bible college the following fall. She felt that was sweet of him but that she'd rather not be under any obligation to him if she could help it, so she wanted to borrow the money and then pay it back after she was out on meetings. Meanwhile, she also asked Brother Stairs if she could borrow the money from the Foreign Missions Department. Brother Stairs responded that he'd brought her request to the missionary board, but had no provision in the manual for such purposes, that they couldn't use undesignated money for her language study even though they understood that the language study would greatly bless the work on the field.

The district board had to say much the same thing. However, the saints in Jerome eventually came through and supplied her need.

Finally we were able to assure her that the district would take over the buildings in Jerome and asked her if she planned to teach for Brother Hurt. Meanwhile, Brother Yadon suggested Billings, Montana, to her and Brother Stairs asked her to meet Brother Beetgee at the Dallas conference to make an arrangement to work with him to evangelize Rhodesia until Northern Rhodesia opened up.

I was able to assuage her feelings by informing her later that year that Brother Tolstad and his mother would move to Billings to take the church there. That eased her mind. Also, her sister, Victory, and her husband would move to Jerome. However, I have not the slightest inkling of where she eventually went, and have lost track of her altogether.

A brother in Lynden, Washington, also wanted to borrow district funds—three or four hundred dollars to get the church built. I wrote back that I didn't know what the board would do but that I'd inform him as soon as possible. On this need, the board did help.

While I labored in the Northwest, I occasionally received letters from Edwin Judd, who was out of the army and now working at Pentecostal Bible Institute in Tupelo, Mississippi. He mentioned that Charlie Yadon had just concluded two and a half weeks of meetings with them in Tupelo. He later notified me that the students would go to DeRidder, Louisiana, for the missionary conference in May.

I also planned to attend that conference, as Brother Stairs was to attend and the foreign missions board would meet, and on my way chose to spend a Saturday night in an El Paso hotel. There I wrote Ernest Moyer a letter in longhand—very unusual for me, since Dad had told me that, given my handwriting, I should either type or not write at all—about the oil and gravel needed for the Bend campground. Ernest Moyer was and is a great man to work with—he works very hard, though now his age works against him.

The next morning I wanted to go into church incognito. You know the saying, "The bigger the briefcase, the smaller the preacher," so I put my small Bible under my trouser belt and beneath my suit coat, then strode into Sunday school hour. Nobody knew who I was—I'd never been there before. Since I was a total stranger, nobody said anything.

After the service, someone came along, shook my hand, and wanted to know who I was, so I had to 'fess up. Then the pastor invited me to his home and took me back to the hotel. From there I took the train that afternoon to DeRidder to meet the foreign missions board.

At that board meeting the Wine case came into the limelight, and no one knew which way things would go. As it turned out, the charges were false, and Brother Wine left the organization.

At that conference, C. S. Currie was also there. Brother Vouga preached a strong message against eternal security, and you could almost see heat waves over Brother Currie's head. I took him out for a walk after service was over to help him cool off, because Brother Vouga had not pulled any punches.

That night Brother Stairs and I slept in someone's home—I don't remember whose. During the night, Brother Johnson called from California to say that Helen White had arrived by plane back from Indonesia. Brother Stairs did not look pleased when he reentered the room from having answered the telephone, and a dark cloud seemed to enter when he did. I did not know why, but found out as he explained to me what had happened. He felt that missionaries should not have any money of their own, because then they might be tempted to leave the field without having any permission from the board to do so. Of course, I could not concur with his attitude, especially since Sister White had gone through the war and the Japanese attack, with shells dropping around her ship. She'd endured a really very precarious and still unstable situation.

Although I sympathized with Sister White and did not share Brother Stairs's opinion, I kept my counsel to myself because I planned someday to go to the mission field.

I've admired Sister White down through the years, how God has been with her and helped her. Though Brother White has now passed on, she still has gone to Indonesia.

Following that conference, I rode back from DeRidder to Tupelo with Brother Judd. Later, on November 13, 1947, he wrote to express appreciation for students who had come from the Northwest and the victories and blessings they had met. (One of those students was Dale Walker, who wrote me that he was finally getting used to

Mississippi weather.) The Northwest students had expressed that they were still committed to PBI until something developed in or nearer their own district. Of course, this did develop later as Conquerors Bible College, founded by Ernest Moyer, who also served as the first president, followed by Orion Gleason, Edwin Judd, Haskell Yadon, Orion Gleason, Ralph Reynolds, John Klemin, and finally Don Fisher. Now, of course, the school has closed, one of those things one cannot predetermine when a school first begins, but it does take place now and then. One can only trust the Lord of the harvest to work things out in harmony with His divine and perfect will whatever the future may happen to hold.

The Salem church, while pastored by Wilbur King, had voted on Wilbur King and Ronald Sittser, the latter winning a majority. We don't want to go into why—Brother King is gone, and Jesus is the same yesterday, today and forever.

When it ended, the church board wrote to me as superintendent informing me of the change in pastorate and saying that they felt they now had a better spirit of fellowship. They wanted to go on record with the United Pentecostal Church as being in favor of a more congenial and harmonious spirit of cooperation than had heretofore been manifest. They also wished to be cleared with W. T. Witherspoon, assistant general superintendent, of any connection or responsibility for a critical letter written by their former pastor.

Brother King, a good man who has passed on to his reward, and whom, along with us all, God will judge in that last, eternal day, had some very pronounced opinions as to what he felt should or should not be, some ideas as to what he thought right or wrong. He was very firm on the message we stand for and unfortunately also on some other things, such as the observance of Christmas. He wouldn't give gifts to anyone, which caused quite an upset even in his own home. Some of these other things did not help him pastor.

Brother Sittser had come out of a Seventh-day Adventist past and spoke against Sabbath-keeping strongly. Within a month of his election, he was battling Sabbath-keeping in Salem.

Brother King left them at Ferry Street and decided to start a new church in his own home. George Eads pastored for a long time on Ferry Street (where my parents had lived in apartments above the mission for quite some time until my mother passed away). The church downtown sent in its application for organizational membership.

Once I had to preside in a Salem church business meeting featuring a conflict between some of the church members and a Brother Barker. This Brother Barker with volatility and volubility expressed his antipathy regarding the pastor, so I felt it my responsibility to ask him to sit down, and did so, which helped the situation. Later, one of the church members commented to my father that she was glad she hadn't been the one I asked to sit down and be quiet. Much of the Salem church history was very much up and down until, as mentioned before, Brother Albert Dillon came.

Brother Sittser invited two guest preachers: Brother Fletcher and Archie Stone. Brother Stone was from Corvallis and would drive around in a mobile home, come to the campground, sharpen knives, do odd jobs of this and that, and thus help maintain his family. A very gifted man in his

255

line of work, he felt a desire to preach from time to time. He loved the Lord and witnessed faithfully.

Brother Sittser also invited the brother who had preached in Rupert against beauty parlors. He would play his banjo and preach, but eventually he backslid. Later, his son pastored in Kenai, Alaska, and told me that his father was playing the violin and banjo for dances in Arizona. Later he moved to Walla Walla, Washington, and in his latter years he came back to God.

Eventually, Brother Sittser almost pulled the Salem church out of the organization into the Latter Rain orbit. The Latter Rain made a lot of headway in those days, now largely replaced by the charismatic movement, also quite prevalent. We thought a lot of Brother Sittser and missed his fellowship, but everyone must sometime stand for what he feels is right and against what he feels is wrong. This was one of those times.

One indisputably good thing Brother King did: he was the father-in-law of Brother Albert Dillon, under whose leadership the Salem church has grown to what it is today.

The Northwestern District wanted to have a prayer and Bible conference. For location, Brother Austin had suggested Brother Rohn's church in Caldwell, Brother Nepstad had nominated Yakima, Brother Sweeten had promoted Rupert, and Brother Sittser had proposed Salem. Of course, we'd need a special conference anyway to vote on whether or not to buy the Bend campground. I asked Brother Rohn about this and complimented his evangelist, Ada Dowe, who came from the Meridian area and had good meetings among our churches even though she was not licensed with us.

The Rohns through the years had a marvelous ministry.

Brother Rohn sang well, especially a song about the Rose, who is of course Jesus—a very touching song—and he sang it beautifully. He and his wife worked hard and ran a Bible college. Teachers with them included Brother Vouga, Brother John Deering, Brother Nutting, and of course, Brother and Sister Rohn themselves. Sister Rohn's lessons on the Tabernacle and other subjects we used in India, finding them a great advantage and help. We do want to pay respect to this compilation of work that they did for the Lord during those years in Caldwell.

At the 1947 general conference, Brother Witherspoon, who had been increasingly ill, passed away.

On December 9, 1947, Brother Rohn's building dedication took place. David Gray, national youth president, spoke. Ellis Scism, district superintendent, as master of ceremonies, was requested to handle the actual dedication, read the appropriate passages of Scripture, and lead the congregation in prayer. Brother Rohn had been district superintendent before me during PCI days and later was again in the UPC.

By late 1947, Sister Stella was back in the Northwest. She had kept in touch from Bay City, Michigan, where she had ministered with Brother and Sister Silvernale, then to Midland, where her parents had offered her an application blank for credentials with the PAJC, since that organization had been revived and had spread, by that time, over four states. It seemed that these brethren still felt considerable antipathy, some to the point of willing "judgment to be brought on others, if God so willed"—perhaps that's one way of putting it—"that the soul would be saved." Why people would feel such vehement antipathy toward each other I found difficult to understand when, to all appearances, we had such unity among our brethren out in the great Northwest.

Sister Stella wanted to come back and asked, "What's open there now, Brother Scism?" I mentioned a number of places: Billings, Montana, had possibilities; Long Valley, Idaho, had a need; Pocatello, Idaho, was there (Clyde Haney had thought of taking it later, but then was killed in an automobile accident); Arthur Egbert had left McCall— quite a few situations.

She eventually settled in Lewiston, where she took over the work and sent in her tithes to the district fund. She settled in and rejoiced that Edna Newcomb would be boarding with her, which would provide some income.

By December, she was impressed with Brother Fretwell and all he wanted to do for God and for His work. Brother Fretwell was a very upright, conscientious brother who no doubt felt something was in the wind, but he actually only visited Lewiston the next month. He went house hunting, then said he didn't feel it was God's will, so he returned to Yakima and to his family. Many ministers change their minds, and how something can cause a mind to change can be surprising. It's not for me to say who is responsible for all these changes, but I do not feel that God always makes these decisions.

Not only did Brother Fretwell not come, but Edna moved to Twin Falls. I wrote to Sister Stella, "I'm sure that you found Brother Fretwell to be every inch the Christian brother I know him to be." I was surprised that he moved to Cowiche. My main desire is to see God's will work out for all in the end.

Brother Fretwell eventually left the fellowship, but each individual must follow what he feels is God's will for his or her life, so it will be definitely contrary to what some others may do and feel, and that quite strongly.

Because Brother Fretwell could not come, Sister Stella said, "They've asked me to stay on as their pastor. I trust for your sake, and the sake of the work as a whole, all will settle down to a steady pull and prayer support for a real progressive move here and God bless each one. I know you desire a real breakthrough and so pray with you to that end."

So that worked out. I had enough troubles of my own— a tonsillectomy. I felt much better after that.

We were to have a conference in Lynden, Washington, but by January 3, the pastor had not heard from me, so he wrote, "I've been waiting to hear from you. . . . I should have written right back. I am terribly sorry, as I was so in hopes that we could get this one." He blamed himself, but I wrote back to clarify with him that Ernest Moyer and I had misunderstood the situation. I'd had to go to Walla Walla for the church dedication and then travel back by way of Bend. Meanwhile, Brother Moyer was preparing papers for his local church building loan. I had talked with him about the meeting and thought that it was all taken care of, but Brother Moyer was so wrapped up in his building program and in such turmoil that the conference had not registered with him. Later on we had the meeting there.

The pastor found it difficult to pay off the loan he'd borrowed from the district, and we reminded him, but I found him in many respects a man worth appreciating in fellowship and ministry. He and his wife were both good, sincere people.

Sometimes we can get mixed up over situations that are

not anyone's fault in particular. Perhaps we prejudge in the beginning, then must overlook certain situations to help solve problems. As I look through letters now many years later, I'm surprised at the efforts we made to help lighten unfavorable situations. The Northwest District Board of the United Pentecostal Church did its very best to help out every situation that came along.

Robert Hammond had trouble in his home due to an accident. Sister Hammond was ill and away in California at the time. I had enjoyed meeting his children, Lewis and Tracy, very much. Later, Tracy married a very fine girl from back East, but at this time Tracy had the unfortunate experience of accidentally shooting his brother-in-law. On January 20, 1948, Brother Hammond wrote back to me:

"Greetings in the precious name of Jesus. Received your fine, consoling letter, Brother Scism, a few days ago. Read it and reread it, then forwarded it to Tracy and Lillian in Grand Rapids, Michigan. I couldn't keep the tears back as I read your letter. We appreciate true friends at a time of sorrow and it seemed the billows would overflow us all, but the blessed Comforter arose within us to live. Lillian sang at the close of the meeting, Sunday, after the accident, 'Jesus Took My Burden and Left Me With a Song.' Her face was shining. Poor Tracy was about to die under it all that Sunday night and a few of us got under a burden of prayer and the Lord lifted him. . . . We do not understand, but someday we will. I know God wants Tracy to consecrate his life in a deeper way and that means Lillian, too. We dedicated him to God when a baby. . . ."

By February 1948, Peter Shebley had asked me to come and visit. I responded that I had to go to Jerome, Idaho, that coming weekend and said, "It is likely that I shall pass through your fair city on the way there. Shall I wave as I go through? Maybe I can have the engineer blow the whistle some extra toots so that you will know that I am one of the little children on board."

By May 1, the Shebleys were saying, "Do you know that we have been here seven months and you have not even paid us one visit?" Less than that has hurt people's feelings in years gone by. Even though I hadn't been there, Sister Shebley said later, "It still remains that Brother Scism is king for the office." They apparently felt that I should hold on to the office of district superintendent until God saw fit to make a change, little realizing, though no less than I, that I would be gone in less than a year.

I congratulated them on having stayed there. After all, they had met with very undue circumstances and some feelings because they did not have a building of their own, but rented a church of another faith, and had very little fellowship with a brother who pastored a Jesus Name church in the area. Then a Baptist sister who had been Sunday school superintendent of the Christian church there received the Holy Spirit, which stirred things up in the community, but God was in it and things worked out for their good and for God's glory. I also informed them that I couldn't come to be with Arthur Hills and Arthur Hodges due to conflicting schedules. Sometimes people have difficulty understanding how things transpire.

They moved to Orissa, California, and I later wrote again to thank them for their efforts, their love, and their work. The Shebleys are wonderful people, not always appreciated as they were worthy of, but God keeps a place in His kingdom for those who really love and serve Him from the depths of their hearts.

Dale Walker wanted a ministerial license. He hadn't received one because he hadn't spoken an average of once per week over a six-month period, so I explained this to him and he later reapplied. He was, in time, district secretary of Oregon District for fourteen years, then later moved to Idaho, where he delivered newspapers. Later he became pastor of First Church in Twin Falls, where Marjorie and I had pastored many years before.

Jim Nicholson, one of our very faithful pastors in McCleary, Washington, did a commendable work for the Lord there. The church had its ups and downs as most churches do, yet the Lord was with him. On my first trip there, in the back of the church there was a stove. It was cold and the good old Washington rain came down. I sat in the middle of my bed with my legs underneath. When Brother Nicholson came into the room and saw my sitting position, he said I would be all right. We've had a great fellowship together.

He procured for our Bend campground many items from an army camp in Washington State. Post-World War II demobilization benefited our church, and we bought the whole list of items at a very reasonable price. Albert Hielke, Joe Smith from Salem, and I drove the truck.

Then we had to install everything at the campground—furnace, sinks—we did a lot of work that year setting up. Not long after that, I resigned and left for India. We had borrowed funds from Alvin Kantola to make the down payment on the camp, and the district later improved it after I left for India.

Later, Jim Nicholson had a stroke and I saw him at Black Rock, sitting in his wheelchair, unable to speak, and being wheeled by his wife here and there about the campground. He greatly loved God with all his heart.

After the Northwest District divided up by states, the Bend campground was sold, but we thank God for all those who received the Holy Spirit there during those early days.

Sister Stella wrote to say that Brother Lawrence was considering being baptized in Jesus' name. That was good news. I trust he had put his tobacco on the altar. God performed a miracle in his life of deliverance and fulfillment of promise.

Stella Peterson was also concerned about the legal status of the Lewiston property and wondered about having it put in the name of the UPC. Her concern was not well-founded—she simply did not understand organizational matters. Each church is self-governing, and therefore as long as her church had trustees, she had nothing to worry about.

Today we have two churches in Lewiston, one pastored by Peter Shebley and the other by Elwin Yadon.

In 1948, while Harry was seeking the Holy Spirit baptism, Bert B. (the whizz-bang evangelist who had said in Oakland, "Last night I could pray them through; tonight I needed them to pray me through") was in revival meetings at the church pastored by Ernest Moyer in Portland, Oregon. During the altar service while Harry was seeking the Holy Spirit, Brother Bert prayed with him. Harry's ballpoint pen dropped out of his coat pocket onto the floor. Brother Bert stopped praying and began to thank the Lord for this pen that had been provided for him. He told the Lord he knew that the Lord had answered his prayer because he had been praying for one. You can imagine the effect that had on a boy just seeking the Holy

Spirit baptism. It disrupted everyone's praying—Harry stopped, Brother Bert stopped, we all stopped. Fortunately, Harry received the Holy Spirit later at the Bend Camp just before we went overseas.

While Harry increased, Marj decreased. Around this time, she endured a dental examination and X-rays. When she took them to her doctor, he couldn't believe what he saw. He then consulted the doctor who had taken the X-rays, and found the results to be all too true. Periodontal disease had set in, and her beautiful set of teeth had to be extracted. We had never dreamed that anything of this nature might happen, nor did we have the finances for it, so she went to the dental school in Portland, where they made her dentures, and that's what she had when we went to India several months later.

Occasionally Brother Stairs would come out to conferences and I would mention India to him. He commented that I should either "put up or shut up." We'd been endorsed back in 1940, but that was before the merger. Brother Stairs now sent us a letter of authorization to raise funds.

In June, Brother Soper, who had heard that I could now go to India, wrote to me, "There's one place that we feel something should be done, and I'm trusting that you will be able to accomplish a real work." God went with us when we went. After many years we left India and came back. There is a work raised up today for God's glory.

By July, everyone at the district conference knew that I was going to India and that my name would not stand for reelection. Brother Goss presided, J. A. Johnson was elected district superintendent, and Ernest Moyer was reelected district secretary. The district board consisted of Brothers

Maulden, Eads, C. H. Yadon, W. R. Wilsie, and Ronald Sittser. Brothers Megrew and Don Austin were not elected that year. Ruby Keyes excellently supervised the children and teenage group activities. I headed out on deputational travel.

Off to India. The Scism family in 1948. Ellis is 39, Marjorie is 43, Harry is 14, and Ferne is 13.

From the 1948 prayer card.
The Scism family.

Wynn Stairs

266

CHAPTER TWENTY

Deputational Travel

*H*arry Judd built us a plywood trailer house on his chicken ranch. It had two double beds. We knew very little about travel-trailer traveling.

The district superintendent of California arranged our schedule in that state, where we had most of our six months of deputation in 1948-49.

In California, we visited relatives and many churches—I can't always recall which ones in 1948 and which in subsequent deputations—1955-56 and 1962-63. In 1948, we stopped to see Isabel and Charles Albert in Redding. She'd led songs many times in Twin Falls. We visited Carmichael, near Sacramento. We visited Oakland—Harry Morse was still there. Possibly in 1948 we visited the Howells in Ontario, California. We deputized in San Diego while the Kinzie party was visiting. David Gray pastored there then and for long afterward.

At the general conference in Long Beach, A. O. Moore said that he would go to South India and that we should go to North India. He also felt that we should not take Harry and Ferne to India. I told him we wanted to go as a family.

At Long Beach, a spit and argue club foamed, that is, formed down by the sea near the auditorium. It had nothing to do with the conference at all, but a lot of our ministers, including C. S. Currie and Oliver Fauss, would go down there and exhaust themselves speaking to the hangers-on. (This is the first time I ever heard Brother Fauss preach.) We'd go down there during off moments in the conference.

We went to the auditorium for the radio broadcast by Charles Fuller of Fuller Theological Seminary. We also visited the zoo, where we rode on a tram. The Vougas, also visiting the zoo, came by and commented that we missionaries had finances to spare for conveyance, while they walked.

One night during the conference, Brother Goss gave me the opportunity to speak, telling everyone that we wanted to go to India and that plans had been made. I had two minutes.

While in Long Beach, we went to see Sister Simmatt, who had gone to Kerala in South India from Mother McCarty's mission in North India. We had decided to go to South India because Brother Moore had not gone to India at all. Sister Simmatt advised us to move to Punalur, a town on a railway where there was a specific house she had in mind. After I got there I couldn't do it, yet we did appreciate her concern for our well-being.

After that, we eventually had some deputational travel

in the Northwest. We spent Christmas of 1948 with Haskell and Ruth Yadon in Twin Falls, where they pastored First Church. We visited almost all the churches in the Northwest at that time, including Idaho Falls, where Don Austin pastored. He also had a shop where he sold used furniture, guns, etc. I bought a chrome breakfast set and a .22 revolver from him.

While in Idaho Falls, I also visited Sherman Howard, my cousin, now a grocery store owner. He had managed an O. P. Skaggs store years before, then had decided to go into business for himself. Now he had a big store. While we visited, we enjoyed him and his family. He gave us a special offering, which we appreciated very much. He had a strong liking for Dad.

We visited Pocatello when Harry Fisher pastored there. Don was a little boy wearing an aviator's cap. He was short when he ended up as well as when he started.

We had a few family matters to care for. Dad and I built a house for him. Naturally, leaving Dad concerned me very much, even though he had lived alone since Mother passed away in 1946. Since my brother and sister-in-law had moved away, he would be alone.

Dad had purchased materials left over from the great flood of the Willamette River, so we hauled those to Salem by trailer and built the house. I did not know then that later my brother would be transferred in his job and would move in with Dad. Ray then paid the cost of the house and Dad built another little house for himself.

About this time, Ike Scism, Uncle Bob's son, said, "Ellis, why go out there to preach to these Indian people? There are plenty of heathen here in America that need preaching to without you taking your family off to India."

He never did give his heart to the Lord, though he'd been there at my first Pentecostal meeting long ago when Brother Frey had prayed for his wife, who had such severe migraines, and which she never had again. He'd shown some tender spots, such as his arrangement of Weston Howard's funeral, but he never, as far as I know, repented or surrendered his heart and life to the Lord. His concern was not for God, but for my wife, me, and our children, Harry and Ferne, going to India. The only time he ever attended church was to a funeral or some other special function—only then would he participate. Later on, he suffered a stroke and was bedfast for a long time until he died.

Many people came to tell us goodbye in Portland. Jean, the daughter of the lady who'd had the nervous breakdown in Tieton more than ten years earlier, came. We did not know from day to day when we would leave because Mr. Dash, the manager of the China Mail, did not know whether part of his cargo, some rice-threshing machines, would come to Portland or to Seattle. Ordinarily, the freighter would not take passengers from one seaport to another on the same coast, but ours did simply because we finally found out the ship had to go to Seattle to pick up the threshing machines.

The evening came when we left Portland on the China Mail, setting sail for Seattle, waving our white handkerchiefs, since that's what we could see in the deepening darkness. Marjorie's mother and my dad were there. This was the last view I had of Dad for six and a half years.

We wended our way down the Columbia River to the bar (the breakwater) and out into open sea. Marjorie was a little seasick when crossing the bar. While on the way to

Seattle, Ferne was playing her accordion on deck, when the inner workings collapsed.

In Seattle, Brother and Sister Kantola took us to a repairer of musical instruments, who fixed the accordion. Also in Seattle, we visited the Megrews. Brother Megrew pastored one of our churches in Seattle, had adopted a couple of girls from Alaska, and was about to leave for a trip to Alaska at the time we visited. He also operated a bakery. I remember how kind he was to us that day—these memories live on and stay with us down through the years. And while at this bakery, we met other friends.

After maybe a couple of days, we sailed on January 31, 1949, from Seattle into the Pacific Ocean toward Japan and to our destination—India.

The great teachers who had taught us in the Salem-Silverton-Howell area and in Oakland, the many experiences we had undergone in Washington and Idaho and across America, and the increasing responsibilities we had overseen in Washington, Idaho, Oregon, and the whole North American Northwest had at least partially educated and, to the extent that they were capable, prepared us for the awesome tasks ahead on another continent far more heavily populated and destitute of the gospel than our own. Having found our Northwest Passage, we now launched a new voyage of discovery to India.